Croner's
MAN
ABSENCE

Written and compiled by the staff
of Croner's Employment Law
Editorial Department

CRONER PUBLICATIONS LIMITED

Croner House, London Road
Kingston upon Thames
Surrey KT2 6SR
Telephone: 081-547 3333

Typeset by Concept Communications Ltd, Crayford, Kent
Printed by Whitstable Litho Ltd, Whitstable, Kent

Contents

Introduction

Absence from work constitutes a significant cost for most employers. Fixed overheads still have to be paid, in many cases wages or salaries continue to be paid. In return, however, the employees concerned make no contribution and may do more financial damage by disrupting production. The importance of the cost cannot be underestimated. A 7% absence rate for an organisation of 500 employees equates to over 8000 working days per year or 16 days per person. If an organisation has an average wage cost of £250 per week, its annual loss is £411,250. Even if absence rates are half this figure, the cost is still substantial to any organisation's profitability.

The costs and consequent damage can obviously be reduced where there are effective policies on absence from work and sensible procedures on implementing the policies. This is not to say that absence can be eliminated. There will always be a certain level of sickness in any company, not to mention annual holidays, special leave and the range of statutory provisions allowing employees to take time off work for maternity leave, medical suspension, trade union duties and activities, public duties, etc.

The purpose of this book is to give managers a straightforward account of the rights of employees in this respect, together with suggestions for controlling the impact of such absences and reducing them as far as possible.

The Scope of the Book

To do this the book is divided into eight chapters:

Chapter 1: Controlling Absence
If absence from work is to be controlled it must be properly measured. Model forms reproduced here make it easy to check on overall attendance problems.

Chapter 2: Illness or Accident

Sickness absence is one of the major causes of absence from work. In this chapter we look at procedures for notifying and certifying sickness absence, controlling it and dismissing people because of ill health. We describe the complexities of the statutory sick pay scheme.

Chapter 3: Pregnancy/Maternity Rights

Ranging from ante-natal care through to maternity pay and leave and dismissal of women on grounds of pregnancy. These are a legal minefield. We aim to remove much of the confusion from this difficult area.

Chapter 4: Statutory Rights

The right to take off is given by law to: trade union officials to carry out certain union duties and duties as safety officers; members of recognised trade unions who take part in their union's activities; employees who take on certain public duties; and employees under notice of redundancy. The legal rules and practical implications of all these rights are covered.

Chapter 5: Special Leave

In addition to these statutory rights many companies provide time off, with or without pay, for a variety of other reasons — compassionate leave, time off for domestic crises or community activities, study leave, time off to attend court, etc. All such examples are illustrated.

Chapter 6: Holidays

We all enjoy taking holidays, but they can become a major headache for managers. This chapter answers such questions as: what happens when an employee is ill during a holiday; can employees be sacked for overstaying leave; what is the rule about paying for bank holidays; must part-timers have the same holidays as full-timers; and a host of other practical issues.

Chapter 7: Lay Offs

Employees may be forced to stay away from work if they are laid off by their employer. This chapter aims to give an essential understanding of the legal and practical implications of this.

Chapter 8: Other Absences

The final chapter of the book examines the issues surrounding three further reasons for absence from work: suspension on medical grounds, disciplinary suspension and imprisonment.

Before going further into this book, two important points must be borne in mind. Firstly, even where the type of absence is governed by legislation, individual companies and organisations will have their own policies and procedures. Secondly, it is impossible, given the length of this book — and incompatible with its purpose — to quote chapter and verse of statutes and case law. Further details can be obtained from the Department of Employment, the Advisory Conciliation and Arbitration Service (ACAS) or from *Croner's Reference Book for Employers*.

1 Controlling Absence

If absence from work is to be controlled the first step is to ensure that it is properly measured. By using the model forms reproduced at the end of this chapter it will be easy to check on the overall attendance problem of employees, without having to go to several records for the complete picture.

Once this information is collected the absence rate can be calculated, per person and per department, by dividing the number of absences by the number of person days and multiplying by 100. For example, in a department with 12 full time employees working a 40 hour 5 day week and six part-timers working a 20 hour week, there will be 75 person days per week. If one employee is away for four full days and two are away for one day each (six person days) the absence rate is $^6/_{75} \times 100 = 8\%$.

Such absence rates can then be used to make a quick check between employees or between departments and any obvious anomalies can be investigated further.

An indication of the cost can be calculated by taking the number of days absent and multiplying this by a daily rate of pay. This will provide an effective guideline for absence control, it will highlight departments with high rates and will focus the managers' attention.

Absence Records

Two examples of an absence record are supplied here, (see Figure 1 and 2) one more detailed than the other. Figure 1 is more comprehensive and provides the opportunity to list on one form a variety of reasons for absence in considerable detail, while the more basic form in Figure 2 covers the main categories of absence. Whichever form is chosen, using one form only for recording all forms of absence enables an overview of an employee's attendance record to be obtained quickly. Due to the detail involved and, in particular, the information as to whether the absences are to be paid or not, it is likely that the personnel or administration department will be in the best position to complete this form. However, copies may be held by line managers for them to keep their own records and cross-refer regularly with the personnel department.

Both forms provide for daily dual recording: this allows details of both SSP and company sick pay payments to be recorded and also makes it possible to enter whether other absences are to be paid or unpaid, by providing for two entries to be made in respect of each day of absence. For example, when employees are away sick the first box can be used for SSP purposes (indicating waiting days, days when SSP is payable and days when it is not), while the second box can be used to indicate whether company sick pay is payable. For other absences, the code can be given in the first box and P or U put in the second box to indicate whether the leave is to be paid or not.

The "remarks" section should be used to give the reason for not paying SSP and for other relevant explanations.

Absence Request Forms

The Absence Request Form (Figure 3) formalises the absence request procedure. This should prevent disputes arising about whether or not the absence was approved. The form can also be used to check that line managers are being consistent in their approval or refusal of absence requests.

On completion by the employee the form should be passed on to the manager for approval. It should then be forwarded to the personnel department so that the employee's individual absence record can be updated.

An additional advantage of using the form is that if employees realise that they will have to fill out the second half of the form if they are absent without approval, they might be deterred from taking such absence. It is therefore a good idea to require employees to complete the form in the presence of their manager and so have to explain themselves, as with the completion of the self-certificate.

A Weekly Absence Return

This form (Figure 4) should be completed by the department head each week and forwarded to the personnel department. It is designed for heads of department as a simple but effective means of monitoring absence levels and of quickly identifying regularly offending employees. It also provides a means of cross-checking other personnel records, eg the Absence Report Form, self-certificate, etc thus enabling the personnel department to identify any absences for which it has no satisfactory explanation.

Figure 1: Absence Record I

Year: _____

Name: _____   Department: _____

Clock/staff no: _____   Start date: _____

Wk No.	Mon	Tues	Wed	Thur	Fri	Sat	Sun	Summary	Wk No.	Mon	Tues	Wed	Thur	Fri	Sat	Sun

Remarks:

KEY:

	X	= No sick pay	M	= Maternity leave	TA	= Territorial Army
	H	= Holiday	C	= Compassionate leave	P	= Paid leave/absence
S = Statutory sick pay	TC	= Training course	TUD	= Trade union duties	U	= Unpaid leave/absence
W = Waiting day	A	= Medical/dental appointment	TUA	= Trade union activities	L	= Late
CS = Company sick pay	AN	= Ante-natal care	PD	= Public duties	I	= Industrial action

8

Figure 2:   Absence Record II

Year: _____

Name: _____   Department: _____

Clock/staff no: _____   Start date: _____

KEY:

	CS = Company sick pay	M = Maternity leave
	H = Holiday	P = Paid leave
S = Satutory sick pay	A = Appointment	U = Unpaid leave
W = Waiting day	AN = Ante-natal care	L = Late

Month	1	2	3	4	5	6	7	8	9	10	11	12	13	14	15	16	17	18	19	20	21	22	23	24	25	26	27	28	29	30	31	Summary

Remarks:

Figure 3: Absence Request Form

Surname	Forenames	Dept/branch	Payroll no.

The following time off work is requested:

Period	From	Day	Month	Year	To	Day	Month	Year

If part of day, beginning at   am/pm to   am/pm

		Working day return date	Day	Month	Year

Reason for absence

☐ Annual holiday   ☐ Death of near relative

☐ Jury/witness duty   ☐ Hospital attendance

☐ Territorial Army   ☐ Appointment for doctor, clinic, optician, dentist, other (please specify below)

☐ Family responsibilities   ☐ Other (please specify below)

To be completed when absence was not approved in advance.

I was absent on (dates): _____

_____

for the following reason: _____

_____

Reason why prior approval was not sought: _____

_____

Employee's signature: _____ Date:_____

Authorisation for time off	With pay; according to entitlement	☐
	Without pay	☐

Manager's signature: _____ Date:_____

Figure 4: Weekly Absence Return

Department: _____   Week ending: _____

Name	Hours or days absent	Reason	Date approved

Manager's signature: _____   Date: _____

This form to be returned to the Personnel Department each Friday by 11 am.

2 Illness or Accident

One of the commonest reasons for employees taking time off work is that they are ill or injured and the problem areas for managers centre on the following aspects:

- notification of absence
- evidence and genuineness of the illness
- the technicalities of occupational and statutory sick pay entitlement.

In this chapter we look at each of these areas in turn.

Notification of Absence

The vast majority of employees are employed on the basis of a fixed working week, so that when employees are unable to turn up for work the company expects them to make contact and explain why they are absent (see notification procedure for statutory sick pay on page 22). On some occasions employees fail to contact employers to inform them of their absence and its reasons. In these cases employers must take reasonable steps to try to contact the absent employees and warn them of the possible consequences (eg loss of pay, dismissal, etc) if they do not get in touch with the company and comply with the notification procedure. Even when the employee does not respond the employer should be sure, before taking action, that this is wilful misconduct on the part of the employee and not, as in some cases, conduct recommended by the employee's advisors or due to any medical condition. For instance in one case the employee was suffering from nervous exhaustion due to strain at work and was being protected from contact with the company by his wife and doctor who felt that such contact would harm his health further.

If an employee frequently goes absent and does not

comply with the company's notification procedures this could, after warning, constitute grounds for dismissal.

In some companies notification is absolutely crucial. For instance, security companies require immediate notification when someone is unable to attend for duties and failure to do so without adequate explanation will result in dismissal. This is because unguarded premises would constitute an enormous problem to a security company, possibly resulting in the loss of a contract. Notification, therefore, is one of their most important operating rules. Other companies formulate notification procedures on the lines of the one set out below.

Absence From Work Including Sickness and Injury: Notification Procedure

- Prior permission must be obtained from the manager to be absent from work, unless the reason for the absence is sickness or injury. Unauthorised absence from work will result in loss of pay unless there are extenuating circumstances.

- Any absence must be notified by telephone or letter to the manager on the first working day of absence.

The Evidence

The next set of problems for managers relates to the question of proving that the person is ill. Most companies require some form of certification, either a self-certificate or a medical certificate, before paying occupational sick pay and statutory sick pay (SSP). (See Figure 5 at the end of this chapter for a model form.) The self-certificate is necessary because doctors will not normally issue a medical certificate during the first seven calendar days of absence. Usually, during this period, the employee will either send in a self-certificate obtained from the doctor or hospital (DSS form SC2) or use an equivalent company-drafted certificate for the same purpose. Many employers have complained that employees just sign themselves off when they feel like it; there is, however, little likelihood of this if an effective policy is adopted, possibly along the lines of the following procedure.

A Procedure on Self-certification

● Employees should be required to complete the self-certificate form in the presence of their managers who then countersign the form, provided they are satisfied that the claim is genuine. This implies that the employees will be interviewed and be asked some pertinent questions — tactfully. It should not simply be a rubber-stamping exercise which is part of the morning routine.

● Managers should ensure that appropriate follow-up measures are taken, such as referral to medical help if there is an underlying health problem, or disciplinary action where details on the form can be challenged, or where short-term, persistent sickness merits further investigation or warning.

Very often this requires the manager to be a little more imaginative in providing solutions to employees' problems. For instance, much absence is caused by the need to deal with problems relating to domestic responsibilities. Special leave may be an answer to dealing with one-off problems, while short-term changes in working hours — for example to enable a child to be taken to school — might take the pressure off an already stressed employee and, incidentally, lessen the amount of time off taken for reasons of ill-health.

The important thing to remember is that a self-certificate, or even a medical certificate, does not provide a cast-iron alibi for absence from work. The employer is quite entitled to challenge it on the basis of other evidence to show that, on the balance of probabilities, the person was not ill. For instance: somebody with a bad back seen on top of a roof fitting tiles; a particular pattern of absence that follows, for example, the school holidays; or an absence when it is known that the rest of the family were on holiday in

Majorca, etc. If the employer forms a reasonable belief that the best explanation for the absence was the alternative activity there would be grounds to terminate employment, having first interviewed the employee, confronted him or her with the suspicions that the absence was not wholly bona fide and asking for an explanation.

After seven calendar days employees can usually obtain a medical certificate from their doctor and there are often company rules requiring a certificate to be provided on a regular basis thereafter. If there are doubts that an employee is ill there are various ways this can be investigated:

- ask the employee for permission to contact his or her doctor for a report. Obtain this permission in writing and ensure that the request complies with the **Access to Medical Reports Act 1988** — see page 27.

- request that the employee sees the company doctor

- where the absence is self-certified and occurs at least four times in a 12 month period, help can be sought from the DSS in checking these absences

- where there is direct evidence that an employee is not ill he or she should be asked to explain those absences in the light of this evidence. Then, if on the balance of probabilities the explanation by the employee cannot be accepted, the employer has the option of stopping any further sick payments or taking disciplinary action which might include dismissal, depending on the seriousness of the case.

Paying Company Sick Pay — Some Problems

It is very common for employers to give an entitlement to sick pay for specific periods of time which often increases with the length of service. Alternatively, payments are made at the discretion of the directors or management with no specific amounts defined. When the payment is a discretionary one and the employer wishes to stop the payment, it is sensible to write to the employee in advance stating the date when the payment will cease.

Another problem frequently arises when an employee

has been ill for some time and then returns to work: does the employee accrue holiday entitlement during this period of absence? The answer, following a careful look at the organisation's terms and conditions of employment and the rules that deal with holidays, is usually "yes". However, some holiday schemes refer to holiday accruing on the basis of weeks worked and in those circumstances holiday pay would not accrue. A further point is that holidays in such cases would only accrue if the employee returned to work — and took the leave — during the holiday year.

Where companies do not have any policy regarding time off work for family or compassionate reasons, it is not uncommon for employees to bring in a doctor's certificate stating that they need time off to look after a member of the family who is ill. This absence does not count as ill-health for the purpose of SSP or occupational sick pay since the employee is, of course, not ill. The company may decide, however, to make a discretionary payment, depending on the circumstances.

Where an employee is off sick and is put under notice to terminate the contract of employment, there is a special provision in law which requires the employer to pay a week's pay for each week of the statutory notice period even if the employee has exhausted or has no entitlement to company sick pay. Obviously employers need to satisfy themselves that the employees are genuinely ill and no doubt medical certificates would be required to substantiate this.

This special rule does not apply when the contractual notice the employer is required to give is at least one week longer than the statutory minimum notice the employer is entitled to receive. In such a case, where the employee has exhausted or is not entitled to sick pay, then nothing is payable during the notice period.

Statutory Sick Pay

When employees are ill they may receive money from two sources: firstly from the company's occupational sick pay scheme which may make payment up to the full normal week's pay, or 50% of that level, or some other round payment while an employee is away ill or injured; secondly from the State's statutory sick pay scheme which the employer administers. This scheme has replaced State sickness benefit in most circumstances and in effect makes the employer paymaster on behalf of the State for social security payments for ill-health.

Company sick pay will be paid under its own set of rules, usually contained in an employees' handbook or in some other similar document, while statutory sick pay is paid under Government regulations. Pamphlets describing this scheme are available from the Department of Social Security.

Statutory Sick Pay Rules

Every manager needs to have some basic knowledge of this scheme in order to explain to employees the payments they will receive from the employer.

The basic rules are best thought of as a series of steps covering:

- periods of incapacity for work
- periods of entitlement
- qualifying days, and
- notification.

Period of Incapacity for Work (PIW)

The period of incapacity for work must last at least four consecutive calendar days. Please note that these can be any days of the week (even if the employee would not normally be required to work on those days), so it is vital to know when the employee fell ill and at what point became fit for work.

"Incapacitated for work" means that an employee is either physically or mentally ill or disabled and cannot perform the kind of work that might reasonably be expected under the contract of employment.

There are other regulations covering circumstances in which employees are deemed to be incapable of work as a precautionary measure against the risk of infection, eg where pregnant women may be exposed to rubella or where food handlers are carrying an infection, etc.

The next important thing about periods of incapacity for work is that they can be linked: PIWs which are separated by eight weeks or less are linked, thus forming one period of incapacity for work.

To summarise, each PIW which links must last at least four consecutive days and any number of PIWs can link in this way, provided the gap between each is no more than eight weeks.

Period of Entitlement

We can now go on to the second step and the next application of rules. The periods of incapacity which we have identified will also be periods of entitlement provided the employee is not excluded from entitlement at the outset. Exclusions operate when, on the first day of the period of incapacity for work (ie the beginning of the first of any linked PIWs), the employee:

- is over State pension age, ie 65 for men and 60 for women, or under the age of 16 years

- is working under a contract for three months or less (separate contracts can be added together provided the gap between them is not more than eight weeks. This exclusion will then only apply if the total length of the contract is no more than 13 weeks)

- earns on average less than the current lower earnings limit (£56 a week from 6.4.93). Earnings limits are changed every April

- has been issued with a linking letter by the local DSS office which indicates that the person has received a State sickness, invalidity or maternity benefit within the previous 57 days

- is new and has done no work for the company

- has a direct interest in a trade dispute at his or her place of employment

- is, or has been, pregnant and is within the disqualifying period (which is the same as either the maternity pay period — see page 45 — for a woman entitled to statutory maternity pay or the maternity allowance period for a woman entitled to State maternity allowance)

- is already in receipt of the maximum entitlement of 28 weeks' SSP in that period of incapacity for work, or a leaver's statement has been provided which shows that 28 weeks' SSP has already been due from the former employer (provided there is a gap of eight weeks or less since the last date of SSP shown on the leaver's statement)

- is abroad in a non-EC country or is detained in legal custody.

In such circumstances an SSP change-over form (SSP1) must be issued and given to the employee within seven days of the fourth day of sickness, or as soon as is practicable, because without it the employee cannot claim State benefit.

Ending of Period of Entitlement

The period of entitlement will end:

- when the employee is fit for work
- when 28 weeks' SSP payment has been made in respect of a period of incapacity for work
- where the employee's linked PIW reaches three years
- when the employee is dismissed or resigns (except where the employer dismisses in order to avoid responsibility for paying SSP)
- when a pregnant employee enters the disqualifying period (see above)
- when the employee is detained in legal custody or goes abroad to a non-EC country.

When the employee is due to come to the end of 28 weeks' entitlement, form SSP1 must be issued at the beginning of the 23rd week of SSP. Where the employer's liability to pay

SSP is due to end for some other reason before the 23rd week, then form SSP1 must be sent to the employee two weeks beforehand.

Qualifying Days

At last we are getting near to deciding what to pay an employee for those days which qualify for SSP payment. We need to know for which days the employee is entitled to receive a payment. These are termed "qualifying days".

Qualifying days must be agreed between employer and employees. They will normally be chosen to reflect the days on which the employee is required to work, or to reflect a shift pattern, or they may be standardised to make life administratively easier. For instance the retail trade often chooses six qualifying days because Saturday working is normal, despite the fact that employees are entitled to a day off during the week.

In any event there must be at least one qualifying day in each week agreed between employee and employer. Usually such matters are covered in the statement of terms and conditions of employment.

Waiting Days

Once the qualifying days are known, the first three days in any period of entitlement are considered to be waiting days — in other words, days for which no SSP will be payable. Do not forget that this is limited to the first spell of absence when there are a series of linked periods. Waiting days have to be served only in the first spell of illness.

Rate of Payment

Current bands of SSP (April 1993) are set out below:

Current Bands of SSP:	
Average Earnings	**Weekly SSP**
Less than £56	Nil
£56 to £194.99	£46.95
£195 or more	£52.50

To find out which band of SSP is payable, average earnings must be calculated by totalling the eight weeks' earnings prior to the beginning of the period of incapacity for work and then dividing by eight. With monthly paid staff two monthly payments are multiplied by six and divided by 52.

It is important to realise that you cannot select the best weeks for calculation and if there are gaps in pay this will depress the average. Perhaps most importantly, the averaging of pay is done at the beginning of a period of incapacity which may in fact be weeks, months or even years before the particular event because of the linking rules. No account can be taken of the contract changing in the intervening time, eg an employee changing from full-time to part-time work or vice versa.

Another important point to note is that in order to find a day's SSP the appropriate rate of weekly SSP has to be divided by the agreed weekly number of qualifying days. Therefore a day's SSP will vary depending upon the number of qualifying days, ie from one whole week's SSP payment for one qualifying day to $1/7$ of a week's SSP payment when there are seven qualifying days. This can be difficult to explain to employees. Furthermore, employees do not receive SSP in addition to their occupational sick pay. The Act of Parliament clearly requires the employer to offset the SSP payment against any other contractual payment made for each day, whatever that contractual payment happens to be, eg holiday pay, retainer, etc.

Any failure to pay SSP, or any complaint arising out of the interpretation of the rules, can be taken firstly under the company's grievance procedure and then to a DSS inspector, who will, in the first instance, try to conciliate between the parties and then give a decision.

Notification and Evidence

Finally, the last qualifying condition for the payment of SSP is that the employee notifies the employer of absence. While employers have some discretion as to the type of rule they operate, they cannot require:

- notification any earlier than the end of the first qualifying day

- notification on a printed form or in the form of medical evidence

- notification more than once in every seven day period.

If the employer's rules are stricter than this, or if no notification rules have been given to the employee, notification made at any time up to the seventh day after the first qualifying day will be acceptable. Many companies do have stricter rules than this and it seems sensible that they should be retained where there are clear operational requirements for earlier notification. However, these stricter rules cannot be applied to the payment of SSP. Where the company rules do comply with the requirements given above, an employee who fails to notify in time can have payment of SSP stopped. Those days off for which there was no notification will not be treated as part of the PIW.

These rules deal only with how the employee tells the employer of sickness absence. The question of evidence which the employee has to provide is also one which must be covered by rules.

Most employers require a self-certification form, either the DSS form SC2 or one they create for themselves, to be presented for the first seven days of the absence; thereafter a medical certificate from a doctor is usually required.

Prior to April 6, 1991 employers were able to reclaim in full from the Government payments properly made by way of deductions from national insurance contributions. From April 6, 1991 most employers are limited to reclaiming 80% of SSP payments made. However, certain employers will be able to recover 100% of SSP in some cases. This is known as Small Employers' Relief (SER).

An employer qualifies for SER if he or she satisfies the following conditions:

- he or she has paid (or was liable to pay) a total of £16,000 or less gross NI contributions (employers' and employees' share) in the last complete tax year before the days for which he or she is reclaiming 100% SSP, and

● the employer has been liable to pay *more* than six weeks' SSP to an employee in a period of incapacity for work (PIW).

Where both tests are satisfied, the employer can recover 100% of any days of SSP payable in the PIW to that employee *after the six week mark*. The SSP due for the first six weeks of the PIW is recoverable at 80%.

Accidents and the Manager

Another important area of the manager's duties involves accidents at work. These may result in significant amounts of time off work and must be notified to the Health and Safety Executive or local authority in certain circumstances.

Major accidents, which must be reported, include those in which someone has died, the fracture of a bone (excluding that of a bone in the hand or foot), loss of sight in one eye, injury requiring immediate medical treatment, loss of consciousness resulting from an electric shock, lack of oxygen or absorption of any chemical substance by inhaling, ingesting or absorbing through the skin and any other injury which results in the injured person immediately being admitted into hospital for more than 24 hours (there is no exemption where the person is kept in hospital purely for observation).

The notification must be done by the quickest practicable means, ie normally by telephone, with a written report on form F2508 (revised) being sent within seven days of the accident.

There is another form of notification which must be made when employees are affected by an accident at work which results in their being unable to carry out their work for three consecutive days. Once again, a written report must be sent to the enforcing authority on form F2508 within seven days of the accident. In this context "days" means calendar days, not days on which the person must be available for work.

The regulations also require the notification of dangerous occurrences. In most cases the person who must complete these forms is the employer. Sometimes employees are injured on other people's sites, eg multi-contractor construction sites and in that case the person who controls the premises must make the notification.

Paying Injured Employees

When an employee has had an industrial accident two questions that are frequently asked are: "Do we have to make any payment to them while they are away from work?" and "Are they entitled to full payment of wages because it is a works accident?" For most employers their obligation to make payment will be set out in their terms and conditions of employment. Additionally there will be a general requirement for all employers to pay statutory sick pay subject to the rules and conditions of that scheme. Consequently most employees will be paid in situations where there has been an accident, provided they have some sick pay entitlement under an occupational arrangement or if they are entitled to SSP. It is common, however, for companies to continue paying employees when they are absent as a result of an accident, even if there is no contractual sick pay scheme, or if the entitlement to sick pay has been exhausted. There is no legal obligation to do this, but in many companies it has become custom and practice. It may be sensible to consider including a clause in employment contracts that, if employees are injured through the negligence of others and recover damages, any company sickness payments must be reimbursed to the company.

Unfair Dismissal Aspects

Whatever kind of ill-health problem results in a poor absence record and no matter how genuine the absence may be, there comes a time when the company's need for employees to attend work regularly is greater than the need to provide secure employment. It is commonly believed that you cannot dismiss employees who are covered by a medical certificate; this is not true. The law on unfair dismissal allows employers to dismiss for reasons of capability and, provided the employer follows a fair procedure, such dismissals are likely to be fair.

Checklist: A Fair Procedure

- The employee should be consulted and told that the absence is causing problems — he or she should know what is going on and what is in the employer's mind.

- The whole matter must be thoroughly and openly investigated.

- The employer should seek medical advice if this is relevant and provided the employee gives permission (see Access to Medical Reports Act 1988 — page 27).

- It is sensible to set time limits for appraising the situation, or a deadline on which a decision to dismiss will be made if the employee has not returned to work.

- If the situation is one of intermittent absences the employee should be told ("warned" — but not a disciplinary warning as this would be inappropriate for dealing with ill health) of the probable outcome if attendance at work is not improved.

- Finally consideration should be given to whether there is any solution to this problem other than dismissal, ie alternative light duties, transfer out of an unhealthy environment, etc.

Long Term Ill-health Dismissals

When an employee is ill for a long time the difficulties of continuing without that employee become increasingly apparent. The question frequently asked is how long must one wait before taking action to terminate employment. The answer to this question depends on many factors: Is he or she a key employee? Is it difficult to get a trained replacement? What is the likelihood of the employee ever returning to work? What is the employee's length of service? etc. It is usually safer to allow the company's sick pay entitlement to be exhausted before taking any decision to dismiss, although this will not of itself guarantee a fair dismissal.

Many employers have an administrative system that is triggered off automatically when an employee has been absent for a set period of time. Such a procedure should ensure that a letter is sent or a visit made to the employee to request permission to contact his or her doctor for a report about the situation. Before any dismissal it is important to try to obtain the current information about the true medical position and it is not sufficient just to ask the employee what the doctor has said. Sometimes doctors do not tell their patients everything. It is better to get the report direct from the doctor but in doing so the employer must comply with the **Access to Medical Reports Act 1988** (see below). An alternative route is to ask the employee to see the company doctor. At this stage it is important that the employee knows why the employer wishes to have the information, ie to estimate for how long the job can be kept open.

Writing to the Doctor

It is not necessary to try to obtain a detailed diagnosis of the employee's medical condition; an enquiry about the nature of the illness, how soon the person will be fit for work again and whether the employee will have to go to hospital to see a specialist, etc is quite sufficient. Will the employee be fully fit on returning to the job, or fit only for light duties? It is also sensible to give the doctor a brief description of the job and working conditions as in some cases the prognosis will be invalid without such background information.

Access to Medical Reports Act 1988

Employers who wish to obtain information about their employees' health must comply with the **Access to Medical**

Reports Act 1988. Under this Act individuals have the right to see medical reports about themselves when these are provided for employment purposes, and supplied by their own doctor. Employers must tell the employees in writing that they intend to apply for the information, and obtain written consent to do this. **The employer must also tell employees that they have certain rights** which include: the right to withhold consent to the application; the right to say they want access to the report before it is supplied; the right to see the report and request amendments; and the right to withhold consent to the report being supplied to the employer. The employer must also explain the effect of certain exceptions under the Act. For instance, a doctor is not obliged to disclose any part of the report to the employee if he or she thinks it is likely to cause harm to the employee's health.

The employer must inform the doctor in writing if the employee wants to see the report, and must let the employee know in writing that the application has been made. At the same time the doctor and the employee must be reminded in writing that the report cannot be supplied to the employer unless either the employee has agreed to it and made any amendments, or 21 days have passed from when the report was requested and the employee has not contacted his or her doctor to arrange to see the report. Further details of the Act are given in *Croner's Reference Book for Employers,* and *Croner's Employment Law.* (See Figures 6–8 at the end of this chapter for model forms.)

If an employee withholds consent to a medical report being sought then the employer will have to go ahead and make a decision about the employee without the relevant information, so the employee should be warned that this will be done if permission is refused.

Access to Health Records Act 1990

The **Access to Health Records Act 1990** goes one step further giving an employer, with the employee's consent, direct access to the employee's health records. This could prove to be a more valuable way of ascertaining an employee's fitness for work than the access to medical reports. Further details of the Act are given in *Croner's Reference Book for Employers*. (See Figure 9 at the end of this chapter for a model form.)

Why Dismiss?

When the investigation is complete, the decision about whether to dismiss or not can be taken, bearing in mind:

- the nature, length and effect of the employee's ill-health
- the employee's previous and likely future service with the company
- the importance of the job and the need for a permanent replacement
- whether it is against the employee's, company's or public's interest to continue employing the person concerned.

Further Discussion

At this point it is sensible once again to meet the employee and discuss the situation. If the employee is not fit enough to be consulted the discussion should take place with whomever is handling his or her affairs, ie a relation or medical social worker.

It may be possible to accommodate the employee on light duties. If there is lighter work available it should be offered to the employee, even if this means lower pay. There is no legal obligation on the employer to create a job, although many employers try to do so for long-serving employees with good records.

In cases where an employee is likely to die within a few months the employer might well decide not to dismiss but to maintain him or her on the payroll, thus allowing the employee's dependants to take advantage of death-in-service grants or other insurance benefits, whilst at the same time permanently replacing the employee since it is quite clear that he or she will not be returning to work.

After considering all the options the employer may decide on immediate dismissal or may set a deadline after which the employee will be dismissed unless work has been resumed. In virtually every case the employer should give notice to terminate the contract, ie paid notice.

Checklist: Long Term Ill Health

- investigate thoroughly
- consult the employee
- seek expert advice (medical) if appropriate
- set time limits for appraising the situation
- explain ("warn" of) the outcome if there is no improvement, and
- consider whether there is any solution other than dismissal.

Intermittent Absences

Absence patterns are not always as extreme as the one mentioned above. Very often patterns of unassociated absences for a variety of reasons are the more usual problems a manager has to face.

The first point which the manager has to decide is whether the absences are caused by genuine illnesses; whether they are evidence of domestic or other personal problems or whether they are symptoms of a disciplinary issue. In the latter two cases, the manager will have to counsel the employee or institute disciplinary proceedings, depending on the underlying problem.

Where it is believed that the cause of absences is ill health it is not really appropriate to put this sort of problem through the disciplinary procedure. It seems unlikely that an employer can warn people and then expect them to make themselves well and not fall ill again but clearly poor absence records are a serious problem for the manager and have to be tackled.

Firstly a fair review of the absence pattern should be

carried out. Care should be taken to ensure that the employee has not been singled out for special attention because he or she is particularly "visible". The absent telephonist is much more noticeable than, say, an employee tucked away in the warehouse. It is also necessary to check whether there is a pronounced pattern to the absence, ie during school holidays, on Mondays or Fridays, etc. It is important to exclude periods of hospitalisation which have actually sorted out the medical problems and therefore should contribute to improved attendance at work.

The next step is to discuss with the employee the absence record. Any written record of this absence rate should be shown to the employee concerned because it will illustrate graphically the amount of absence occurring and, probably for the first time, the employee will realise that it is excessive.

It might be sensible to check that there is no underlying problem at home or at work. There may be an underlying ill-health problem in which case the employee should be persuaded to see a doctor.

The employer should then explain to the employee what is a reasonable standard of attendance, perhaps based on what is being achieved by other members of the department or company as a whole. A reasonable period of review should be set in order to see if the employee can improve. At the same time the employee should be told what will happen if the pattern of absence continues in the same manner, eg a further review period or dismissal with notice. Of course, it is a good idea to confirm the whole conversation in writing to the employee. For further details and example letters see *Croner's Guide to Managing Fair Dismissal*.

Figure 5: Company Self-Certificate

Name: _____ Department: _____

Job title: _____ Payroll no: _____

A.

Date and time illness began: _____ Date fit for work: _____
(including non-working days) (including non-working days)

First notification to: _____ Notification date: _____
(give method of notification and name of person notified)

B.	C.
Reason for absence:	Did you attend hospital YES/NO
	clinic YES/NO
	your doctor YES/NO
Please describe symptoms:	Did you receive medication either from
	(i) your doctor YES/NO
	(ii) self prescribed from chemist YES/NO
Give detals of accident:	If you are still away from work due to illness when are you likely to be fit for work?
	Date: _____

I understand that if I provide inaccurate or false information about my absence it may, depending on the circumstances, be treated as gross misconduct and result in my summary dismissal from the company.

Signature: _____ Date: _____

Manager's remarks (including date of return if known):

Signature: _____ Date: _____

Figure 6: Medical Report Consent Form

I. To: _____ (employee's name) Date: _____

On behalf of _____ (company name)

I wish to obtain a medical report from your doctor/Dr _____

for the following purposes: _____

_____

_____

Authorising signature: _____

Position in company: _____

II. Employee rights under the Access to Medical Reports Act 1988

1. You can ask to see the medical report before the company receives it. This request for access can be made either:

   (a) to the company when you grant us permission to obtain it (in which case we will tell the doctor of your request, and let you know when we apply for the report);

   (b) direct to the doctor at a later date, but before the report is supplied to the company.

2. If you ask to see the report:

   (a) you must contact the doctor to arrange access within 21 days of the company applying for the report, otherwise the doctor can give the report to us without showing it to you and without your consent. (Under 1(b) above you must contact the doctor within 21 days of notifying that you wish to see the report);

   (b) having seen the report, you can ask the doctor (in writing) to amend anything which you think is incorrect or misleading. If the doctor does not agree, a statement of your views will be attached to the report at your request;

   (c) provided you have seen it, the report will not be given to us unless you give the doctor your consent.

3. You will not be entitled to see any part of the report which:

   (a) the doctor believes could seriously harm your physical or mental health, or that of others;

   (b) indicates the doctor's intentions in respect of you;

   (c) reveals information about another person, or the identity of someone who has given the doctor information about you (unless that person consents or is a health professional involved in your care).

4. The doctor will tell you why access to the whole or part of the report is refused. Your rights of amendment will apply only to the disclosed part of the report. The doctor will only give the report to the company with your consent.

5. You do not have to give the company permission to obtain a medical report. (However, the inability to obtain up-to-date medical information may affect decisions made about your employment with the company.)

6. You may ask to see any medical report relating to you which the doctor has provided for employment purposes in the last six months (if prepared on or after 1.1.89). Such a request should be made to your doctor.

- -

III. **This part is to be completed by the employee and returned to the employer.**

To: _____ From: _____

Company name: _____ Address: _____

_____

_____

I hereby consent to the company requesting a medical report from: _____ (doctor's/

consultant's name) of_____

_____ (address)

I have been informed of my rights under the Access to Medical Reports Act 1988. *I wish/I do not wish to see the report.

*Delete as appropriate

Signed: _____

Date: _____

Figure 7: Medical Report Request

To: _____ (doctors' name) Date: _____

Address: _____

_____

On behalf of _____

_____ (company name and address)

I am writing to request a medical report from you on _____

_____ (employee's name and address),

a patient of yours.

As we require the report for employment purposes, its provision is subject to the Access to Medical Reports Act 1988. The employee in question has been informed of his/her rights under the Act and enclosed is a form on which he/she has signed consent for this request to be made.

We would be grateful, therefore, if you would answer the following questions for us regarding the employee's state of health, bearing in mind the nature of his/her work, which is as follows:

As the employee has asked to see the report, the Act requires that it must not be supplied to us by you unless:

(a)   he/she has seen it, agreed to its being supplied to us and, should he/she believe it to be incorrect or misleading, has had it amended or attached a statement to it to that effect;

or

(b)   21 days have passed from the date we requested the report without the employee contacting you to arrange access to it.

We will, of course, be prepared to pay for the report — subject to the above-mentioned time-scales — would appreciate an early reply; a stamped addressed envelope is enclosed.

Thank you for your co-operation in this matter.

Yours sincerely

Name:
Position in company:

Figure 8: Notification of Medical Report Request

To: _____ (employee's name)

From: _____

Company name: _____

This is to advise you that, further to you granting permission, our request for a medical report from your doctor is

being made on _____ (date).

As you have asked to see the report, the doctor must not supply it to us unless:

(a)   you have seen it, agreed to its being supplied to us and (should you believe it to be incorrect or misleading)
       have had it amended or attached a statement to it to that effect;

OR

(b)   21 days have passed from the above date without you contacting the doctor to arrange access to the report.

Signed: _____

Date: _____

Figure 9: Access to Health Records Request Form

I. To: _____ (employee's name)   Date: _____
    On behalf of: _____ (company name)

    I wish to obtain access to your health records from your doctor or other health professional (name and address):
    _____

    for the following purposes: _____

                                              Authorising signature: _____
                                              Position in company: _____

II. **Employee rights under the Access to Health Records Act 1990**

1. The Access to Health Records Act 1990 enables you as a patient to request in writing access to your health record or part of your health record from a holder of that record.

2. The application may also be made by a person authorised by you, in writing, to make the application on your behalf.

3. The holder of the health record will usually be your own doctor or may include the company doctor, or other health professional. Such other ''health professional'' may include:

    (a) a registered medical practitioner;

    (b) a registered dentist;

    (c) a registered optician;

    (d) a registered pharamaceutical chemist;

    (e) a registered nurse, midwife or health visitor;

    (f) a registered chiropodist, dietician, occupational therapist, orthoptist or physiotherapist;

    (g) a clinical psychologist.

4. Following a request for access the record holder must allow the applicant to inspect the record, or part of the record, and if required supply a copy.

5. The period within which access must be allowed to the record is:

    (a) 21 days from the date of application where the record or part of the record was made in the 40 days preceding the application, or;

    (b) 40 days from the date of application where the record is made more than 40 days before the application;

    (c) if the holder needs further information to identify the patient or be satisfied that the applicant is entitled to apply, then the record holder has 14 days to ask the applicant for clarifying information. In this case the 21 day period begins on the date that information is provided.

6. The holder of the record may refuse access to any part of the record which:

    (a) the health professional believes could seriously harm your physical or mental health, or that of others;

    (b) reveals information about another person, or the identity of someone who has given the doctor or health professional information about you (unless that person consents or is a health professional involved in your care).

7. The Act does not entitle access to be given to any part of a record made before November 1, 1991 unless it is necessary to make subsequent parts intelligible.

8. You do not have to give the company permission to obtain access to your health records. (However, the inability to obtain relevant medical information may affect decisions made about your employment with the company.)

- -

III. **This part is to be completed by the employee and returned to the employer.**

    To: _____   From: _____
    Company name: _____   Address: _____
                                                      _____
                                                      _____

    I hereby consent to the company requesting access to my health records from: _____ (doctor's/
    health professional's name) of: _____

    I have been informed of my rights under the Access to Health Records Act 1990.

                                                      _____
                                                      _____

3 Pregnancy/Maternity Rights

The vast majority of managers are likely to have pregnant women working for them at least once during their working lives. Most people are aware that such employees have certain rights to time off from work but are not always sure exactly what those rights are. A pregnant employee may be entitled to time off for ante-natal care, to maternity pay and may have the statutory right to return to work after maternity leave — all of which are subject to different qualifying conditions. Added to these rights are the contractual rights which some employers give these employees (both intentionally and unintentionally). No wonder people get confused!

Ante-natal Care

The term "ante-natal" refers to the period before the baby is born, when a woman is actually pregnant. However, there may be a period prior to that when the question of time off with regard to pregnancy might arise. As a manager you may be approached by an employee (either male or female) seeking time off work to attend a hospital or a clinic for treatment for infertility. Such employees have no right in law to be given paid time off for such appointments, nor is it likely that they would be absent from work due to sickness. Employers may well be sympathetic in such cases and allow the employee to take time off, but should beware of setting a precedent for future claims which they might not want to follow.

In most cases, however, the question of time off will first arise with a pregnant employee when she has to attend for ante-natal check ups. Paid time off for ante-natal care is a right to which all pregnant employees are entitled by law. It does not depend upon the number of hours worked or length of service.

If it is the first appointment the employee does not have to produce any written evidence that she is attending for ante-natal care. However, for subsequent appointments she can be required to produce a certificate of pregnancy and an appointment card or some other documentary proof that an appointment has been made.

So, what is ante-natal care? Well, it is not defined by the legislation, other than by way of stating that the employee's attendance must be on the advice of a doctor, midwife or health visitor. It is almost certain that what should definitely be included are the visits to the hospital or doctor which pregnant women are expected to make for checks on their weight, blood pressure, state of health, etc.

For most women, their first visit to the ante-natal clinic is somewhere between the eighth and twelfth week of pregnancy. Then, if the pregnancy is straightforward and there are no complications, the pregnant woman is likely to have to visit the clinic once a month. In the last two or three months of the pregnancy she will have to go every two weeks and, in the final stages of pregnancy, every week. This might be seen as the "standard" in terms of ante-natal clinic visits and is often the minimum required by medical advisors.

Besides this, however, many pregnant women — particularly first-time mothers — are encouraged to attend ante-natal classes. These are often held during the day and cover such subjects as relaxation, caring for the baby, coping with labour, health during pregnancy, etc. They are not usually compulsory but are generally regarded as a good idea.

What is Ante-natal Care?

So where does the employer draw the line between ante-natal care which entitles the pregnant employee to paid time off and that which does not? The pregnant woman must not be "unreasonably refused time off during working hours to attend for ante-natal care". Since the importance of the ante-natal clinic visits are stressed so much by the medical profession, the "standard" number of visits described above will undoubtedly count. The situation with the classes is less clear cut. If the employee cannot produce evidence to show that she is attending on medical advice, she may be refused paid time off. However, if she can produce a statement from her doctor that the classes are an essential part of her ante-natal care an employer may well have to think more carefully before rejecting her claim.

The fact is, however, that even if it is legitimate ante-natal care, paid time off might still be refused on the basis of reasonableness. There are a number of different factors to take into account when assessing reasonableness. To start with, many pregnancies are not "standard"; for one reason or another the pregnant employee might have to visit the ante-natal clinic more frequently than once a month. Yet even if she has only to visit on the "standard" number of occasions, the number of times she has to be absent for ante-natal care might pose real difficulties for the manager in terms of covering the work. Then there is the length of time that each visit takes; the clinic might be in a difficult location, not readily accessible by public transport, and the woman will almost inevitably have to queue for some time. This means that one appointment could easily write off a whole morning or afternoon.

Summary: Ante-natal Care

- Infertility treatment — no right to paid time off — **not** equivalent to sickness.

- **All** pregnant employees are entitled to paid time off for ante-natal check ups — no qualifying service is required.

- Evidence may be required after the first visit.

- 8-12 weeks into pregnancy — check-ups start. Thereafter 1 per month.

- After 6-7 months of pregnancy — frequency will increase to 1 visit per fortnight.

- After 8 months of pregnancy — weekly visits to doctor likely.

More may be required on medical advice.

How Much Time?

What can be done to try to get over the problem? An employee may be able to make appointments outside working hours. This may not be very easy for a full time day worker but for part time staff and shift workers there should be more possibilities. If an employee refuses to co-operate in this without good reason it may be perfectly reasonable for the employer to refuse her paid time off.

If the problem is one of location, with the employee spending a large proportion of the time off travelling to and from the clinic on public transport, it might be cheaper and more worthwhile for the employer to pay for a taxi for her or to arrange for a colleague to give her a lift. It is important to remember that what is reasonable time off for one pregnant employee might not be for another. The crucial question is, can employers show that they have been reasonable? Each case must be dealt with separately and the needs of the employee weighed up against the needs of the company. One possibility may be to require the employee to take the time off as annual holiday.

What an employer must not do, however, is to tell her she can have the time off — but without pay. A pregnant woman's right to time off for ante-natal care is a right to time off *with pay* and she must be paid at the appropriate hourly rate (ie the amount she would have been paid had she not taken the time off). If a woman is either unreasonably refused paid time off for ante-natal care or given the time off but without the proper pay, she can complain to an industrial tribunal and get compensation. It would be up to the employer to show that the refusal was not unreasonable.

Contractual Rights

Some employees may also have extra contractual rights in respect of time off for ante-natal care — possibly the granting of paid time off to attend relaxation classes, regardless of whether they are the result of medical advice.

Ideally, any contractual rights like this should be set down in writing for all to see. That way the employees know exactly what their rights are and everyone should be treated consistently. It may be that as a condition to getting any extra rights, employers require employees to let them know as soon as possible that they are pregnant. The result should be a benefit for the employee and early information for the manager to enable forward planning to cover maternity leave where necessary.

There is, however, the danger of granting contractual rights to time off for ante-natal care unintentionally. One or two employees may be given paid time off to attend relaxation classes without question, perhaps by another manager. This could set a precedent which would make it very difficult to refuse another employee in the future. If the employer wants to keep the right to do this on a discretionary basis, it should be put in writing. Then each case should be looked at on its merits. Whatever happens, do not try to contract the employee out of her statutory rights as this will have no effect.

Company Policies

Some companies have detailed written ante-natal policies and require early notification for another reason. Namely, that there are health and safety risks for pregnant women. Some substances, for instance, which are quite safe for people to work with under normal circumstances, can be potentially very harmful to the unborn child. One problem with this is that the first three months of pregnancy are usually the time when most damage can be done. This is why employees need to be urged to notify any pregnancy early on. Obviously, some employees do not know themselves until they are several weeks (or even months) pregnant. The important thing is that the employees' health and safety at work is the employer's responsibility. If you think some of your female employees might be put at risk in this way, you should do all you reasonably can to warn them of the dangers and impress on them the importance of notifying the company as soon as they think they might be pregnant. If the dangers are very great, it might even be worth making arrangements to transfer women to "safe" work if it is known that they are trying to become pregnant.

VDUs are a particular source of controversy when it comes to health and safety and pregnant employees. Expert opinion seems to be that there is no danger for pregnant women working with them. Recent research suggests that spontaneous abortion is no more likely amongst women working with VDUs than amongst the general population.

Employers should also consider a pregnant woman's fitness for work in terms of their own liability should she suffer damage. For instance, a pregnant woman whose job normally involves carrying bulky objects through swing doors, up and down stairs, etc is likely to be at risk of injuring herself and/or her unborn child. In such a situation it may well be held that the employer should have foreseen such a risk and so could be liable to be sued for damages.

(In some industries the provisions on suspension on medical grounds cover some of the cases described above, see page 107.)

Absence Problems

It is often the case that managers, who have never had to deal with pregnant employees, hear stories about all the difficulties they cause. Then they are faced with their first "case" and wonder what all the fuss was about. It is true, however, that from time to time problems such as illness, poor attendance and capability do complicate dealings with a pregnant employee. Managers are often unsure how far to go when tackling them and not without good reason.

As explained in the first chapter (see page 13), the fact that an employee is genuinely ill does not mean that if his or her work is being affected the employer cannot take action. The same principle applies with pregnant employees although it is important to bear in mind an overriding risk of sex discrimination which is explained later in this chapter.

Taking illness first, it may be connected with the pregnancy or it may be totally unconnected. (Pregnancy itself is not regarded as an illness.) The employee should not be any less entitled to company sick pay than if she had not been pregnant or than if she had been a man. If this does happen it could amount to indirect sex discrimination.

The fact is that pregnant women do have extra

protection from unfair dismissal. It is automatically unfair to dismiss an employee just because she is pregnant or for a reason connected with it. Before the European sex discrimination developments described later, the only exceptions were if being pregnant stopped her doing her job properly, or if it would have been unlawful for her to continue the job, eg on health and safety grounds (see above). Even if one of these reasons could be shown, suitable alternative work had to be offered if it was available.

This is why employers have tried to argue that illness and/or absence prevented a woman doing her job. However, industrial tribunals are always very wary when dealing with pregnancy dismissal cases. They tend to be suspicious of employers' motives and look long and hard at employers' actions and the reasons for them.

Some points to bear in mind include the following:

- pregnant employees whose absence is suspected as not being genuine should be dealt with in the same way as any other employee (see page 14)

- an employee with a difficult pregnancy may be advised to rest at home by her doctor. This is unlikely to come under time off for ante-natal care but should be treated as legitimate sickness absence unless there is evidence to suggest otherwise

- some employees are advised by their doctors (at various stages of the pregnancy) to stop work until after they have had the baby. Faced with this situation, the employer may well be able to show that this makes it impossible for the woman to do her job. Before making any decisions, the details should be confirmed by her doctor. Dismissal could lay the employer open to claims of sex discrimination (see below). Alternatively, she could continue in employment until the time when her maternity leave (if she was entitled to it) would have started. At that point arrangements may be made with her to give the employer all the proper notice, etc and take up her statutory rights (see below). The second course of action is generally easier, as it means the employer does not have the potential problem of an unfair dismissal or sex discrimination claim. It may cost the company nothing if the employee has no entitlement to company sick pay, yet leave the employer free to take on a replacement to cover for her

- if the employee's state of health is an issue, try to get medical opinion where appropriate and available.

The end of the absence problem is often likely to come when the employee has the baby or goes on maternity leave.

Sex Discrimination

It has already been pointed out that an employer may unlawfully discriminate on grounds of sex by treating a pregnant woman differently from others. Note, however, that special favourable treatment of women in connection with pregnancy or childbirth is not unlawful discrimination against men.

One area where unlawful discrimination can creep in is that of dismissal. The extra protection for pregnant women against dismissal applies only to those who qualify to claim unfair dismissal. In other words, a pregnant employee with less than two years' service cannot claim unfair dismissal, whether on grounds of pregnancy or not. However, what she might be able to claim is unlawful sex discrimination, for which she needs no qualifying service. What she would have to show is that a man in similar circumstances (they obviously cannot be identical!) would have been treated differently, ie not dismissed. For example, a pregnant woman who is sacked because of her absence might be able to show that a man of similar service with the company, suffering from a medical condition which was causing the same level of absence, would not have been dismissed. If she can and the tribunal accepts her argument, the dismissal will be unfair on grounds of sex discrimination. If the company can show that they would have treated such a man in the same way, the dismissal should be fair. This is known as the "comparative" approach.

However, employers should also note that the European Court of Justice has held that under EC law, dismissal due to pregnancy amounts to direct sex discrimination. In this context no justification is acceptable and the "comparative" approach described above cannot be relied upon.

In effect this protects all women irrespective of their length of service from being dismissed on grounds of pregnancy. As a result of the adoption of the EC Directive on Pregnant Women at Work, substantial revision of the maternity provisions contained in the **Employment Protection (Consolidation) Act 1978** will take place. The main addition will allow for all pregnant women to take 14 weeks' maternity leave and resume work. No service qualification is required.

Statutory Maternity Rights

There are two main statutory maternity rights:

● statutory maternity pay (SMP)

● statutory right to return to work after maternity leave.

Qualification for these entitlements is slightly different. However in both cases a very important date is the date the baby is due, the expected date of confinement (EDC). This is the date the employee's own doctor will be working to and will be included in her pregnancy record. Ideally the employer needs the certificate of the EDC called a Mat B1 but this is not issued until the employee is about six months pregnant because doctors can change their minds about when a baby is due as the pregnancy progresses. You can ask to see the certificate once it has been issued, but before this there should be a note of the EDC on the employee's record.

For both maternity leave and SMP purposes employers need to be able to work out the date of the beginning of the 11th week before the expected week of confinement (EWC). Maternity "weeks" run from Sunday to Saturday and the week during which the baby is due (ie the week in which the EDC falls) is the expected week of confinement. Count back 11 weeks from the beginning of the EWC and you have that all important date! For example if the date of confinement is 8.11.93, the beginning of the 11th week before the week of confinement is 22.8.93.

Statutory Maternity Pay (SMP)

SMP is paid by the employer who then claims it back from

the State. SMP is payable to any eligible pregnant employee, an employee being a person whose earnings attract liability for employers' Class 1 national insurance contributions. The employee does not need to be married to receive SMP, nor does she have to intend to return to work. Eligibility depends on a number of factors:

● the pregnant employee must have been continuously employed for at least 26 weeks (irrespective of the number of hours worked) ending with the 15th week before the EWC. This 15th week is called the qualifying week (QW). She must be employed during the QW, but does not need to be employed for the full week

● average weekly earnings for the previous eight weeks ending with the QW must be no lower than the lower earnings limit for paying NI contributions in force during the QW (from April 1993 this is £56.00 per week)

● the employee must still be pregnant at the 11th week before the EWC, or have already been confined

● she must have stopped work due to pregnancy or confinement

● she must provide her employer with notice of her maternity absence and evidence of her EWC.

Notification

She must give 21 days' notice (in writing if requested) of her intention to start maternity absence. If less notice is given the employer can decide whether or not to accept the employee's reason for this. If there is any dispute it may be referred to the DSS to decide. The employer must see evidence of the EWC, usually the Mat B1. Any other evidence will not be valid for SMP purposes if it has been issued before the 27th week of pregnancy. Evidence should normally be produced no later than the third week of the employee's maternity pay period, but in certain circumstances this may be extended to no later than the 13th week.

Maternity Pay Period

SMP is paid for 18 weeks. This period is called the

maternity pay period (MPP) and can start anytime from the 11th week to the sixth week before confinement. SMP cannot start earlier than the 11th week before the EWC, and if the woman works later than the sixth week before the EWC she will lose some SMP although any "lost" weeks will be ones for which the lower rate would have been payable. SMP will also be lost if she is taken into legal custody, goes outside the EC, dies, or works for her employer during the MPP or for another employer after the birth, whilst she is still in her MPP.

Payment of SMP

Tax and NI are deducted from SMP. The employer may offset SMP against any contractual maternity pay benefits. SMP is normally paid on the usual pay days, but can be paid as a lump sum. However, the employer may have problems then recovering overpayments if the woman becomes disentitled to SMP during the MPP.

Rates of Pay

There are two rates of payment — known as the higher rate and the lower rate. The higher rate is paid to women employed for at least two years at 16 hours or more per week or at least five years at between eight and 16 hours per week ending with the QW. The rate is nine-tenths of the woman's average weekly earnings (calculated over the eight weeks up to the QW) or the lower prescribed rate of SMP whichever is the greater. This higher rate is paid for the first six weeks of the MPP.

The lower rate of SMP is the prescribed weekly rate (£47.95 from April 1993). It is paid for the remaining 12 weeks of the MPP to women who qualify for the higher rate. It is also paid for the full 18 weeks of the MPP to those women who qualify for the lower rate only, ie those who have been continuously employed for at least 26 weeks but less than two years ending with the QW.

Recovering SMP

Employers can claim the full amount of SMP paid, by deducting it from NI contributions due to the Inland Revenue. An amount equal to secondary NI contributions payable on SMP can also be reclaimed (4.5% for 1993/94). Employers must keep records of SMP payments and medical evidence provided by employees.

Early Confinement

It is not unknown for a baby to arrive unexpectedly early and the SMP rules do account for this. The employee will still qualify for SMP as long as she would otherwise have had adequate service, and notifies the employer of the date of the baby's birth within three weeks.

Less happily, if the baby is stillborn before the end of the 24th week of pregnancy, SMP is not paid although the employee may be entitled to SSP. If a stillbirth occurs after the start of the 16th week before a woman's EWC, SMP should be paid.

Dismissal before the QW

The employer cannot avoid liability for SMP by terminating a pregnant employee's contract for that purpose.

Maternity Allowance

Pregnant employees who do not qualify for SMP may be entitled to maternity allowance which is claimed from the DSS. For further information see *Croner's Reference Book for Employers*.

Contractual Maternity Pay

There is nothing to stop employers paying employees who leave to have a baby on more generous terms than the statutory minimum — either in the amount paid, the length of the period for which payment is made or the qualifying period (eg one year instead of two for the full amount). These terms should be spelt out clearly in a written document and made available on request.

Maternity Leave and the Statutory Right to Return

The following flow chart illustrates an employee's statutory right to return (Figure 10).

Figure 10: The Statutory Right to Return

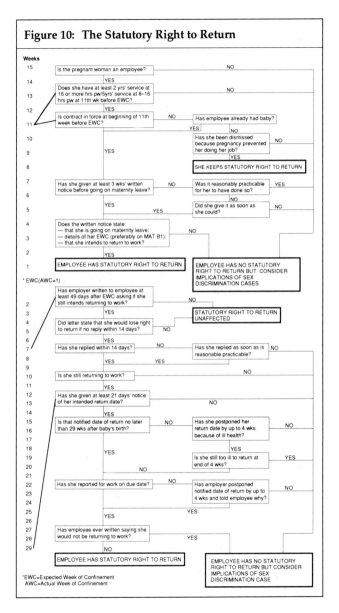

Weeks

15	Is the pregnant woman an employee? — NO
14	YES
13	Does she have at least 2 yrs' service at 16 or more hrs pw/5yrs' service at 8–16 hrs pw at 11th wk before EWC? — NO
12	YES
11	Is contract in force at beginning of 11th week before EWC? — NO — Has employee already had baby?

YES — NO

Has she been dismissed because pregnancy prevented her doing her job? — NO

YES

SHE KEEPS STATUTORY RIGHT TO RETURN

YES

Has she given at least 3 wks' written notice before going on maternity leave? — NO — Was it reasonably practicable for her to have done so? — YES

YES — NO

YES — Did she give it as soon as she could? — NO

Does the written notice state:
— that she is going on maternity leave;
— details of her EWC (preferably on MAT B1):
— that she intends to return to work? — NO

YES

EMPLOYEE HAS STATUTORY RIGHT TO RETURN

EMPLOYEE HAS NO STATUTORY RIGHT TO RETURN BUT CONSIDER IMPLICATIONS OF SEX DISCRIMINATION CASES

* EWC(AWC=1)

Has employer written to employee at least 49 days after EWC asking if she still intends returning to work? — NO

YES

STATUTORY RIGHT TO RETURN UNAFFECTED

Did letter state that she would lose right to return if no reply within 14 days? — NO

YES

Has she replied within 14 days? — NO — Has she replied as soon as is reasonable practicable? — NO

YES — YES

Is she still returning to work? — NO

YES

Has she given at least 21 days' notice of her intended return date? — NO

YES

Is that notified date of return no later than 29 wks after baby's birth? — NO — Has she postponed her return date by up to 4 wks because of ill health? — NO

YES — YES

Is she still too ill to return at end of 4 wks? — YES

NO

Has she reported for work on due date? — NO — Has employer postponed notified date of return by up to 4 wks and told employee why? — NO

YES — YES

Has employee ever written saying she would not be returning to work? — YES

NO

EMPLOYEE HAS STATUTORY RIGHT TO RETURN

EMPLOYEE HAS NO STATUTORY RIGHT TO RETURN BUT CONSIDER IMPLICATIONS OF SEX DISCRIMINATION CASE

*EWC=Expected Week of Confinement
AWC=Actual Week of Confinement

49

The earliest date that maternity leave can start is the 11th week before the EWC. To get statutory maternity pay the employee must give the proper notice, as described above. If she wants to be able to come back to work after she has had the baby, she must give at least three weeks' notice but this time it must be in writing (unlike notice for SMP where oral notice will do unless the employer requests otherwise) and she must state that she intends to come back to work. She can always change her mind later and decide not to come back. In such a case, her effective date of termination would be the date that she advises her employer in writing that she does not intend to return. If she does not keep her right open when she gives notice, she will lose her right to come back and will not be able to change her mind. This means that managers are often faced with the problem of not really knowing what the woman is going to do. Many pregnant employees keep their options open just in case "something goes wrong", eg a stillbirth, but have no intention of coming back otherwise. The best approach is generally to try to talk to the employee and find out her true intentions orally. As long as she keeps her right to return in writing she will not lose out.

Again, as described under Statutory Maternity Pay (see page 46), if it is not reasonably practicable to give three weeks' notice, she must give as much notice as possible in order to keep her rights.

Of course, it is always possible that the pregnant woman might miscarry, or give birth prematurely. Will she still have maternity rights in those circumstances? In some cases she will, in some she will not. It all hinges on the word "confinement". Statutory maternity rights are given to women who are away from work because of pregnancy or confinement. For these purposes, "confinement" means the birth of a living child, or the birth of a child whether it is living or not after 24 weeks of pregnancy. A woman who miscarries before she is 24 weeks pregnant will not have these rights. A woman who miscarries or has a stillborn baby after 24 weeks will still be entitled to all the rights she would otherwise have had. If a living baby is born, regardless of how far into the pregnancy, its mother will also have all the usual rights (this can be as early as the 24th week of pregnancy). Bear in mind that this last situation can override the usual rule of not starting maternity leave earlier than 11 weeks before the EWC. The actual date of confinement will take precedence.

Starting the Leave

Forgetting what are generally extreme cases, such as those just described, most pregnant employees start their maternity leave on or after the 11th week before the EWC. Note that they do not have to go at 11 weeks before, that is just the earliest date. Only if she is incapable of doing her job properly after that time can an employer really start suggesting to an employee that she should begin her maternity leave. Otherwise she can continue working right up until the day she has the baby if she wants to and is able. If an employer tries to force her to go earlier than she wishes she might be able to claim that she has been unfairly dismissed. The choice of leaving date should really be hers.

A pregnant employee who leaves at the earliest possible date will have the right to take approximately 40–44 weeks' maternity leave. In some case it might be less, in some it might be more. She has the possibility of 11 weeks' leave before the EWC and 29 weeks after the actual date of confinement (ADC). In other words, the date the baby is actually born decides how much maternity leave in total its mother can have (and very rarely do the EDC and ADC exactly coincide!). If the baby is early, the mother still gets only 29 weeks' leave afterwards, even if she has not had her full 11 week entitlement beforehand. Equally, if the baby is late, the 29 week rule still applies, giving the mother more than 40 weeks' leave available in total.

Preparing for the Return

It is clearly important, then, to find out from the employee when the baby is actually born, so that you work forward from the right date. In many cases the manager will probably hear through the employees' colleagues if she does not come forward with the information herself. Alternatively, ask around if you do not hear, or contact the employee or her family direct. In any case, a manager should always check a hearsay date with the employee; but do try to avoid contacting her too soon after the EDC. There is nothing worse for a pregnant woman than to be asked "have you had it yet" when she is two weeks overdue and heartily sick of the whole thing!

Once it is known when the baby was born the latest date when the employee can come back to work can be calculated. She must return before the end of 29 weeks beginning with the week when she has the baby.

For example, if the ADC is 3.5.93, the employee should return to work by 20.11.93.

As soon as 49 days have passed since the beginning of the originally notified EWC, the employer can write to the employee and ask her if she still intends coming back to work. The employer must not write earlier. In the letter the employee must be told that she has 14 days in which to reply and that if she does not do so within that time she will lose her right to come back to work. One of three things is likely to happen:

- no reply at all. You can now work on the basis that she has lost her right to return. The same applies if she replies saying that she does not wish to retain her right or does not want to return to work

- she replies in the 14 day period saying she does want to return to work and so retains her right

- she says that she wishes to return to work but does not say this within the 14 day period. In this case, she will not lose the right to return provided it was not reasonable for her to reply in time — perhaps because she was away from home and did not receive the employer's letter until the time limit had already expired.

Exercising the Right to Return

If she has retained the right to return, she must exercise it by giving to her employer three weeks' notice, in writing, of the date on which she intends to return to work — the notified date of return (NDR). This must be no later than the end of 29 weeks starting with the week in which the baby was born.

The right to return means that she has the right to go back to her old job on terms and conditions of employment no less favourable to her than those which would have applied had she not been away on maternity leave.

Postponing the Return

The employee may postpone her date of return by up to four weeks if she is able to produce a medical certificate stating that she is unfit to return to work in the following two ways:

● if she has already given her employer an NDR, she must give her employer the certificate and notice of postponement before the NDR

● if she has not given an NDR, the doctor's certificate must be given to the employer before the end of the 29 week period.

In either case, if she is still not fit to return to work at the end of the four week period, she loses her right to return.

Similarly, the employer may postpone the date of return by up to four weeks, provided the employee is notified of the postponement, given the reason for it and the date on which she may return. Finally, the return may also be postponed if there is an interruption of work, eg a strike which makes it unreasonable for the woman to return. In such a case, if she has already given her NDR, she simply has to turn up for work when normal working resumes. If she has not notified a date, she must do so within 28 days of the end of the interruption of work.

Refusal to Re-employ

If an employer refuses to allow a woman to return to work, even though she has fulfilled all the necessary conditions, this will count as a dismissal and she will be able to make an unfair dismissal claim to an industrial tribunal. The date of dismissal will be held to be the NDR and the employer's reason for refusing to allow her to come back will be the reason for the dismissal. For instance, suppose that an employer has employed a temporary replacement for a woman on maternity leave, who turns out to be more efficient than the absent woman, and the employer decides to keep the temporary worker in preference to allowing the woman to return. This would almost certainly count as unfair dismissal as the woman seeking to return would probably have had no prior warnings and no opportunity to improve.

If the refusal to allow the woman to return was because her job was redundant, she would still be able to make an unfair dismissal claim and would be likely to succeed in her claim if:

- she was selected for redundancy just because she was on maternity leave

- there was a suitable alternative vacancy and it was not offered to her as an alternative to redundancy.

There is an exception to the right to return for very small businesses. Where, immediately before the woman went on maternity leave, there were no more than five people employed (including employees of any associated employers) and the employer can show that it is not reasonably practicable to allow the woman to return to work, there will not be an unfair dismissal.

Part Time Work

Many women who previously worked full time might want to return to work in the same job but in a part time capacity. Whilst this is not covered by the legislation itself, an appeal tribunal has in the past held that failure to consider this option may well constitute sex discrimination. This does not mean that employers have to allow women to return on this basis regardless of the disruption it might cause: rather, they must consider whether this is a reasonable option in terms of covering the job efficiently without causing undue difficulties.

Dismissal During Maternity Leave

From time to time employers want to dismiss employees while they are away on maternity leave. The best advice that can be given is: don't! The reason for this is simple. In such a case the woman would be able to bring an unfair dismissal claim but — and here is the rub — such a dismissal would not take away her right to exercise the statutory right to return and if this was refused she could make a second claim. Even where it is known that the woman will not be allowed to return to work, because of redundancy for instance, no action should be taken until she gives her NDR.

Contractual Rights

In some cases, a woman will have contractual rights to return to work as well as statutory rights. Where the contractual rights are more favourable, for example if she is allowed to take one year off work after the ADC, she may choose to exercise either right. However, she will still lose her right to return if she fails to comply with either the statutory provisions or any conditions attached to her contractual rights.

Employers need to be aware that a contractual right might be given unintentionally. For instance, a woman who is not entitled to statutory maternity leave stops work to have a baby. Shortly after the birth she receives a letter from her employers saying she cannot return to work and enclosing a cheque representing two weeks' pay in lieu of notice. In such a case it must be assumed that her contract continued until the time she received the letter — otherwise there would have been no need for her employers to send the letter — that letter would be treated as dismissing her and so she would be able to make an unfair dismissal claim provided she had the necessary qualifying service.

Conditions on Return

On return to work the woman has the right to go back to her old job on terms and conditions of employment no less favourable than if she had not taken maternity leave. This means that, with regard to pension rights, seniority and so on, her employment prior to taking the leave must be treated as continuous with her service on returning to work.

Where holidays are concerned suppose, for example, a woman returns from maternity leave on July 1; if her holiday year runs from January to December in the year she returns she will be entitled to half her normal annual entitlement.

No Statutory Rights

The conditions which govern the calculation of continuous service for the purpose of qualifying for statutory rights specifically cover the case of women who leave work because they are pregnant but who do not qualify for statutory maternity leave. If they return to work within 26 weeks of leaving, their service will be deemed to be continuous: the periods before and after the absence are added to the number of weeks they were away, even when no arrangements are made when they leave that they will return. It should be stressed, however, that in such circumstances there is no statutory obligation on employers to re-employ. If the woman has left because of her pregnancy, it is up to the employer whether she should be offered her job back and, if so, whether this should be within the 26 week time limit. However recent European developments change this as will the provisions contained in the **Trade Union Reform and Employment Rights Bill** (see page 45).

Career Break Schemes

Many employers, recognising the value of their experienced female staff and not wanting to lose them to other employers, operate career break schemes. These schemes allow women to leave work to have children and stay away for a considerable length of time, for instance up to five years. When they return to employment it is in their original post and grade with updating training given where necessary.

The scheme may only be open to women who have been in service for a certain length of time, and of a certain degree of seniority. If the employer operates such a scheme, it is important that the details about it, and who qualifies are clearly specified.

4 Statutory Rights

"You can't stop me taking time off. The law says I can —
and get paid for it!"

Many employers find themselves from time to time
faced with insistent employees demanding to be allowed
time off — perhaps to attend to union business or to go on a
course. In order to respond sensibly and with authority to
such requests, employers need to know just what the law
does say about people taking time off work. A good starting
point is to ask an employee to complete a request form (see
Figure 11 at the end of this chapter).

In fact the occasions on which the employer is obliged by
legislation to allow time off with or without pay are strictly
limited. Many companies imagine, for example, that
Territorial Army leave and jury service must come under
this heading, but that is not the case. (These situations are
examined in the next chapter.)

Apart from the law relating to maternity, which has been
covered in the previous chapter, employees have rights to
time off in the following four well-defined areas:

Rights to Time Off

- to carry out certain trade union duties and activities
- when acting as safety representatives
- to fulfil public duties
- when under notice of redundancy.

Needless to say where employment law is concerned, there
is more to these broad categories than meets the eye and a
rather more detailed explanation is necessary.

Eligibility

In order to benefit from any of these rights to time off (except those covering trade unions) employees must work for 16 or more hours per week. In the case of redundant employees, they must also have completed two years' service but the other rights do not depend on qualifying service.

The entitlements also apply to part time staff who have worked for eight hours a week (but less than 16) for five years or more.

Trade Unions

In law a clear distinction is made between trade union duties and trade union activities — broadly, the former relate to officials of trade unions and the latter to the ordinary members. Another useful guide is that duties are concerned with industrial relations activities between the employer and the trade union representative whereas activities are normally concerned with internal trade union government and/or administration. In both cases a trade union has to be "recognised" by the employer in order for its officials or members to qualify. A union is "recognised" if the employer bargains with it, to any extent, on matters such as terms and conditions of employment.

Employees who are officials of independent trade unions recognised by the employer are entitled to reasonable time off during working hours to carry out their duties or to undergo training.

Trade Union Duties

Statutory time off with pay during working hours is allowed to union officials only where the union duties are concerned with either:

- the negotiation of matters in respect of which the union is recognised by the employer, or
- duties that the employer has agreed the union may perform on behalf of the employees.

In either case the duties must be connected with one or more of the following matters:

- terms and conditions of employment, or the physical conditions in which any workers are required to work

- engagement or non-engagement, or termination or suspension of employment or the duties of employment

- allocation of work or the duties of employment as between workers or groups of workers

- matters of discipline

- membership or non-membership of a trade union

- facilities for officials of trade unions, and

- machinery for negotiation or consultation.

The ACAS Code of Practice on Time Off for Trade Union Duties and Activities provides guidance on granting time off.

Some organisations have agreed procedures with the relevant unions which go into some detail about how time off requests by union officials should be handled. If that is the case managers should familiarise themselves fully with the arrangements agreed.

One point worth noting is that an official who is taking part in industrial action is not entitled to be paid for it. However, if the individual is simply representing the strikers in relevant negotiations with management but not personally taking part in the action, time off with pay should be permitted.

Shop Stewards

Time off for trade union duties is only given to an accredited shop steward or union representative but this begs the question: who is eligible to be such a representative and does the employer have any say in the matter? In many cases, the initial agreement made between the employer and union which granted recognition rights will set out conditions which must be fulfilled by the union representative. Such conditions are likely to include requirements as to ballots of union members and may state that only employees with a minimum length of qualifying service may stand for election. (See also Safety Representatives, page 63.)

Training of Union Officials

In order to be able to carry out their duties effectively and successfully, trade union officials need to undergo industrial relations training from time to time and the law obliges an employer to allow time off with pay for this purpose.

The training must be relevant to the carrying out of the official's duties and those duties must be ones for which time off would be given. In addition, the training must be approved by the TUC or by the official's own union.

The ACAS code recommends that officials should have time off for initial basic training as soon as possible after they are elected or appointed. In addition, it suggests that time off should be allowed when a need has been identified for further training relevant to officials' industrial relations duties.

Such a need may occur when an official gains new areas of responsibility, where alterations in structure have taken place, or when changes to industrial relations legislation are in the pipeline.

None the less the course must be directly relevant to the duties of the official, or to duties which could arise in the course of future negotiations. The employer is entitled to ask to see details of the course content and, if it is inappropriate or too general to be of use to the official in the course of his or her duties, time off may be refused. Much may depend on the level in the union hierarchy that an official has reached. A first-rung shop steward is unlikely to need an intensive course on pay structures if there is a joint negotiating committee which deals with such issues. A basic course will be irrelevant for a seasoned campaigner.

The ACAS code advises that unions should normally give at least a few weeks' notice of the names of officials they would like to see go on a particular training course. The number absent at any one time should have regard to the employer's requirements in operating the business smoothly.

Trade Union Activities

Activities meriting reasonable time off work are clearly separated from duties as far as the law is concerned. The activities covered are those of members of an independent trade union which is recognised by the employer; an employee who happens to be a union member but whose union is not recognised has no statutory entitlement to time off. Under this heading, the organisation does not have to pay the individual for absence.

Examples of the activity which qualifies for the granting of time off are given in the code of practice:

- taking part, as a representative, in meetings of official policy-making bodies, eg the executive committee or annual conference

- representing the union on external bodies, eg industrial training board committees

- voting at the workplace in union elections

- attending urgent meetings of members which do not adversely affect production or service.

While taking part in industrial action is expressly excluded, the code does point out that, on occasion, a group of employees directly affected by such action (but not taking action themselves) may need to ask for management's agreement to time off for an emergency meeting. In such a case, it may be in the company's interests to allow such time off if the meeting is likely to stop the dispute spreading to other areas.

How Much and When?

The legislation stresses that time off must be reasonable in all the circumstances. Of course, one manager's view of reasonable may vary quite considerably from one employee's view. To provide some guidelines it is appropriate to look at the factors which should be taken into account when deciding the reasonableness issue.

First and foremost, employers are responsible for

maintaining their production and services; unions, for their part, have a responsibility to bear that fact in mind when asking for time off. Requests should be made as early as possible, giving details of reasons for the application, how long the person will be away and where he or she will be during that time.

Once management is satisfied that the request does come within the compass of time off permitted by law, the operational problems must be looked at. If all the shop stewards want to hold a union meeting on the busiest day of the week in a bakery, for instance, that is likely to be considered unreasonable and management would be entitled to ask for a postponement to a less crucial day.

A mass exodus for training which could result in safety cover being affected would obviously be unacceptable to an employer, who may reasonably ask the union to reduce the numbers involved.

Where mass meetings of members during working hours are concerned, the code of practice makes the point that management and unions should, wherever possible, agree on a convenient time which minimises the effects on production, such as towards the end of a shift or either side of a meal break. Granting permission for such meetings during working time will also help to ensure that meetings are more representative of the workforce as a whole.

As well as the timing, the amount of time off has to be reasonable. Constant requests for officials to attend two week courses are clearly likely to result in serious disruption if granted; again a sense of proportion should prevail.

Time off granted for other purposes, for instance public duties (see later in this chapter), may also be taken into consideration when assessing whether a request is reasonable or not.

It is important to emphasise that every request for time off needs to be looked at in the light of circumstances prevailing at that particular time. "No two days are ever the same" may be a cliché but is none the less a true and apt statement. Situations can change overnight and a reasonable refusal to allow time off at a certain time of year may turn out to be an unreasonable refusal a month later if current circumstances have not been taken into account.

Safety Representatives

There is another aspect of the law relating to time off concerning organisations which recognise trade unions, ie regulations which cover time off with pay for safety representatives who have been appointed by independent, recognised unions.

The law states that safety representatives should normally have 2 years' service within the company. Although the ACAS code goes on to state that where this is not reasonably practicable 2 years' service in the industry would be appropriate. This is the only area where an employer may have some say in the appointment of safety representatives because the law leaves the manner of appointment to the trade union concerned.

Employers must permit such representatives to take as much time off work as is necessary to carry out their duties and to undergo training. The absences must also be paid.

In general terms, safety representatives are there to act as a bridge between employer and employee in promoting health and safety. More specific functions include the following:

Safety Representatives: Specific Functions

- investigating possible hazards and dangerous occurrences at the workplace
- examining the causes of accidents at work
- looking into employee complaints about health and safety matters
- making inspections of the workplace and of relevant documents
- attending safety committee meetings.

Where training is concerned, the Health and Safety Commission has drawn up a code of practice which gives general guidance. In parallel with the "trade union duties" code, it suggests that as soon as possible after appointment safety representatives should receive basic training through a course approved by the TUC or by the appropriate union (although this approval is not an absolute requirement in law); further training should be given where the representative has special responsibilities or where additional training is necessary to cope with changes in circumstances or legislation.

Employers, too, should make sure their own in-house training is provided on the hazards of the particular workplace and on how they organise and make arrangements for health and safety.

When attendance on a course is requested by the union, the code recommends that at least a few weeks' notice should be given to the employer, who is entitled to see a copy of the course syllabus. Basic training should be designed to give safety representatives an understanding of the company's safety policy, their role and that of safety committees and trade unions in relation to health and safety matters at work. It is important, in particular, to clarify the interests of the group of employees which they are directly representing.

For the newly appointed representative, too, new skills must be taught: what to look for when carrying out a safety inspection; where to find essential information on safety matters, etc.

When considering time off for safety matters an employer will clearly need to adopt a flexible approach so that a representative can respond quickly to situations which need urgent attention or investigation. It is helpful, however, to try to reach agreement in advance with the unions on the amount of time off likely to be required for "standard" activities such as regular workplace inspections and safety committee meetings.

Payment

When an employee is granted time off for union duties or to

act as a safety representative, payment must be made by the employer. The general rule on payment is that officials should be paid the amount they would have received if they had worked during the time off. The calculation becomes rather more complicated when pay varies with the amount of work done, eg piece work. In that case the average rate of pay that the person would have had if he or she had worked during the absence should be given (or a fair estimate made). If it is not feasible to use any of these methods, an average can be made of the pay of someone else in comparable employment.

If a night-shift worker, in order to fulfil union duties, carries out duties on the day shift, that official should be paid the night shift allowance for that period. This follows the principle that officials are entitled to be paid as if they are still doing their ordinary work. Similarly, if a lay-off situation arises when a safety representative is absent on a training course, there is still an entitlement to average hourly earnings even though, had he been working at that time, only guarantee payments would have been made.

Certain other queries may arise, the most common being whether or not overtime pay should be taken into account. If the employees concerned are bound under their contracts to work overtime, any overtime they would have done if at work should be included in the calculation. If, on the other hand, the overtime is not contractual, it should not form part of the amount given.

It can happen that only part of a training course or meeting is used for union duties. In these circumstances employers are obliged to pay only for that proportion of time off. (Of course, the remainder may constitute union activities which attract unpaid time off.) There is no entitlement to be paid for the day or for time off in lieu if a training course takes place on a rest day because there is no statutory requirement to pay for time off when training is undertaken at a time when the official could not otherwise have been at work. An employer needs to deal with this carefully. For example, it would seem appropriate to compensate a night worker who attended a course during the day whereas for a course attended at the week-end it would not be appropriate to pay.

Disputes

With common sense on all sides the granting of time off will normally create few problems, particularly if employers are able to reach agreement with their recognised unions on broad guidelines.

None the less, disagreements over what is reasonable and over whether payments should or should not be made are bound to arise from time to time. Any complaints should be raised through an agreed procedure specifically set up for the purpose (if there is one) or else through the organisation's normal grievance procedure.

Where the matter is still unresolved the union official or safety representative may bring a complaint to an industrial tribunal that the employer failed to permit reasonable time off or that proper payment has not been made. Such a claim must be made within three months of the employer's "failure", if reasonably practicable.

If a tribunal finds that the complaint of failure to allow time off is justified it has to make a declaration to that effect and can award any compensation which it feels is just and equitable in the circumstances. The tribunal must award the pay due to the employee in a situation where time off for union or safety duties has been allowed but no pay received.

Public Duties

Organisations which are staffed by public-spirited people frequently receive requests for time off to enable employees to play an active part in wider community affairs.

Where the law is concerned employees are entitled to take reasonable time off without pay to carry out certain public duties. The employer is obliged to grant time off to an employee who is:

- a justice of the peace
- a member of a local authority
- a member of any statutory tribunal

- a member of a National Health Service trust, a regional, area or District Health authority, Family Practitioner Committee (Family Health Service Authority) or Health Board

- a member of the governing body of a grant maintained school, a higher education corporation or an educational establishment maintained by a local authority

- a member of a water authority or river purification board.

The kind of activity which requires time off under this heading is attending meetings of the body concerned, or performing other duties which are necessary for the body to function properly. For example, a local authority chairperson, apart from attending regular meetings, may need to go to the authority's offices to attend to matters which crop up in between the actual dates of the scheduled meetings.

Before agreeing to time-off requests for public duties, an employer may take into consideration the following factors: how much time is required for the performance of the duties; how much time the employee has already taken off either for public duties or for trade union duties or activities; and the effect that the employee's absence will have on the running of the business. However, simply rearranging an individual's duties (eg by tacking extra hours on to adjoining days) so that he or she is expected to do the same work at different times would not be regarded as allowing time off during working hours.

It should be relatively easy to get a clear idea from the individual or from the offices of the authority itself of roughly the amount of time the person will need to spend carrying out public duties. Naturally this will vary with the workload of the body concerned and the importance of the employee's role in it. It is up to the employer then to decide how much time off it is reasonable to grant, given the particular circumstances.

If there is a dispute and the matter is referred to an industrial tribunal, matters such as the ability of the company to cope with absence at a busy time, the nature of the employee's job and whether cover can be provided will all be taken into account, assuming they amount to genuine reasons for not allowing time off. Nevertheless, a tribunal will balance the employer's arguments against an employee's reasonable requirements. A tribunal may well look askance at an employer in a large organisation who refuses reasonable time off to someone who is not a key worker and, as with trade union duties and activities, compensation may be awarded where a tribunal considers it just and equitable.

On the whole, however, the law encourages a spirit of compromise in these matters. There is no code of practice on public duties to provide guidelines and so it is very much up to the parties concerned to come to sensible arrangements.

It is worth noting that, although people have no right to be paid if they carry out public duties, employers are, of course, free to pay employees, if they wish to.

Redundant Employees

Anyone who has been employed continuously for two years or more (working at least 16 hours per week) and who is under formal notice of redundancy is entitled to reasonable time off during working hours to look for a new job or to make arrangements for training for future employment. Note that the right is not confined to people who receive statutory redundancy pay, so that an 18 year old, for example, who has two years' service must be allowed to take time off even though redundancy pay is not due.

A redundant employee does not have to give details of interviews or appointments beforehand and time off does not need to be confined to going to interviews. For instance, an employee may need to go along to a job centre or employment agency during working hours — or even to look through job advertisements in the newspapers at a local library.

If an employer unreasonably refuses time off during the

Figure 11: Request for Statutory Time Off Work

Name:_____ Clock/staff no: _____

Department: _____ Job title: _____

I wish to take a leave of
absence on (dates or times): _____

---

for the following purpose: _____

Signature:_____

Approved by: _____

Date: _____

To be completed when statutory time off was not approved in advance.

I was absent on (dates): _____

---

for the following reason: _____

Reason why prior approval was not sought: _____

Signature:_____

Date: _____

To be completed by the personnel department:

Absence code: _____ No. of days absent:_____

Paid/Unpaid: _____

notice period, a redundant employee can make a claim to an industrial tribunal. Compensation may be awarded by the tribunal, up to a maximum of $2/5$ of a week's pay for the entire notice period.

The Employer's Position

In summary, the basis for dealing with statutory time off requests is that of applying "reasonableness". To this end, agreements made in advance with unions or individual employees over the likely amount of absence can be helpful in giving guidelines and minimising disputes. In the context of rights to time off under the law, an employer's discretion is strictly limited; the next chapter deals with situations allowing the employer much more freedom.

5 Special Leave

We have so far considered a number of situations where employees require time off work, many of which are governed by statutory provisions which set out guidelines on particular entitlements. However, as some managers know only too well, employees can come up with all sorts of reasons why leave of absence is required and, naturally, the law does not fully cater for all of them. Each of us, at some time or another, is likely to need "special leave", the term often applied to time off work which as such has no (or only a limited) statutory basis.

Consider the following situations: "I was just about to leave for work when the dishwasher flooded the kitchen with water. Can I have the day off to see to it?"; "The driving test centre has just rung me to say they've had a cancellation and my test is now scheduled for next Thursday. Can I have some time off to mug up on the highway code?"; "I've just received a letter from the police asking me to attend court from the 27th onwards to give evidence about a road accident I witnessed."

As a manager, you will often be faced with this sort of request. Do you have to grant the leave? If so, how much and should this be with pay or without pay? Will granting the leave create a precedent and lead to more problems? This chapter attempts to answer these questions by looking in depth at the more common requests for leave of absence which may not be catered for adequately by the law.

Compassionate Leave

One of the more common needs for special leave is where this is requested on compassionate grounds. Usually compassionate leave is associated with the more traumatic experiences in life which, unfortunately, all of us are liable to face from time to time. A bereavement or the serious illness of a member of the family will normally warrant leave of absence on compassionate grounds, as indeed might the break-up of a marriage or other close personal relationship, or an employee's financial or housing problems.

In general, compassionate leave is not a prescribed entitlement, being granted in most cases at the discretion of the employer. However, in some cases (notably in larger organisations) clear policies have been established which set out specific entitlements depending on the reasons for which leave is required. In these circumstances the employer may be bound to observe these entitlements where they form part of the employee's contract of employment, so it is always as well to check whether or not particular requests for time off must be answered by reference to the contract.

Even where a contractual entitlement to compassionate leave exists, the amount of time off permitted is likely to vary from organisation to organisation, as indeed will the reasons for which it is granted. However disruptive the immediate absence of an employee may be, most managers will be sympathetic to an employee's need for time off on the death of a close relative, especially where the employee is responsible for funeral arrangements or is particularly distressed. Likewise, the serious illness of a member of the family, or perhaps a case where an employee's child has gone missing, is likely to receive a sympathetic hearing. Other cases may not be so clear cut. The employee who is in arrears with the local bookmaker may well find that a request for "compassionate" leave to deal with the problem receives short shrift from the employer. The important point is to exercise sensible judgment; it may not be such a bad idea in certain circumstances to allow your gambling employee to "take a few days off and get things sorted out!", particularly where further investigation shows that the individual is a compulsive gambler who needs specialist help or is so heavily in debt that it is affecting job performance.

The amount of time off that should be granted and whether this should be paid or unpaid is again normally open to discretion. Even where the contract of employment stipulates a specific entitlement it is as well to consider the particular circumstances of each case. It may be that the time off permitted by the contract is insufficient for the employee's purposes and, in a genuine case, may need to be extended, or the company may feel that it is appropriate to pay the employee even when no right to payment exists. Clearly the nature of compassionate leave sometimes dictates that these matters are best played by ear. If you rely too much on a specific entitlement of, say, one day's unpaid compassionate leave in the case of serious illness in the family, this will not do much to promote good staff relations where, for example, the employee's spouse is in intensive care and likely to die at any time and the employee has no other leave entitlement remaining. Equally, whilst it may be necessary to agree initially to an open-ended arrangement, it is just as important to monitor the situation in order to ensure that the concession is not abused.

Inevitably, there may well be cases where employees are content to remain away from work on full pay *ad infinitum*. Fortunately, these cases are somewhat rare but they do occur from time to time and it is important that the position is kept under review. Much will depend on the reasons why leave has been granted but it can sometimes be necessary to consider transferring the employee from paid to unpaid leave or to make tactful enquiries in respect of the employee's continued absence. It is most important that the issues are investigated before any decision is taken on whether to curtail the time off. In some cases this may involve weighing the needs of the business against the individual's continuing absence and adopting a fair but firm approach.

Domestic Crises

In addition to time off requested on "compassionate" grounds, employers may be faced with requests for special leave to deal with everyday domestic crises which are not of the "compassionate" nature. These can be remarkably varied and will often be made on very short notice. The more common household disasters usually head the list — burglary, burst water pipes or fire in the home are likely to lead to a request for immediate leave of absence to deal with the problem. Other occurrences might include the fact that the employee's child minder has failed to turn up and immediate time off is needed to look after the children, or the employee needs the day off to be in when the telephone or gas engineer, etc arrives to fix a household appliance. Oddly enough, some employees are of the opinion that these domestic issues will automatically qualify for paid leave. This may be so if the contract permits it. However, this would be unusual and in the vast majority of cases the issue is again down to the discretion of the employer.

In deciding whether time off should be granted and, if so, whether this should be paid or unpaid, you should taken into account the urgency of the issue involved, whether the employee has given or could reasonably have given any notice of the need for time off and, of course, the effects of the time off on the business. In most cases where time off is granted, it will be appropriate to insist that employees take the time as part of any holiday entitlement they may have, or to agree to the request on condition that they make up the time on return to work.

Community Activities

Not surprisingly, employees enjoy other pastimes in life apart from fulfilling their contractual obligations to their employer and occasionally employees' participation in activities in the community can impinge on their employment and lead to requests for special leave.

Some employers, keen to foster good relations with outside agencies and improve the company's standing in the community, actively encourage employees to participate in external activities and are therefore willing to grant time off for various purposes.

Territorial Army duty: Time off for Territorial Army duty is a common request from some employees who may be required by the reserve force to undertake periods of duty or training. Since this is a voluntary activity there is no legal basis for time off work for this purpose unless, of course, the contract so provides. However, most employers are prepared to grant the leave, though it may be appropriate to require employees to use their holiday entitlement. The question of payment is again at the employer's discretion.

Where individuals have used up their holiday entitlement extra leave (paid or unpaid) may be given if the employer so wishes.

Secondment: In some cases the initiative for leave of absence may come from the company itself. Some organisations are prepared to second staff to take up positions on bodies which do not qualify for the statutory time off rights granted under s.29 of the EP(C)A (see Chapter 4), eg voluntary regulatory boards for industry, community organisations such as charities, or units set up to provide particular services to the public such as community information services, etc. Firms of solicitors, for instance, often second staff to law centres or advice bureaux in this way. The secondment of staff can be beneficial to both parties. Not only does it give the employee the chance to participate in community activities but it enables the employer to enhance the company's standing in the community and can provide a useful means of dealing with short term bottlenecks in career paths where such problems occur.

The question of who pays employees during periods of secondment will usually depend on the terms of the agreement between the seconding employer and the organisation to which the employees are being seconded.

Medical Matters

In an earlier chapter we looked in detail at employees' rights to time off and pay in respect of sickness absence. But what about those cases which may not fall readily under the rules of the statutory sick pay scheme or the company's own sickness provisions? For instance, what do you do if employees say they need the afternoon off to see the optician for an eyesight test; or employees tell you that they have booked into a health farm for a week? Do these situations qualify as sickness? Some would say "yes", as undoubtedly they are matters relating to an employee's health. However, it may equally be contended that sickness rights apply only to situations where an employee is "incapable of work", thus potentially excluding such matters from the scope of sick pay schemes. Naturally, this can be a grey area and will usually boil down to the definition of "sickness". Certainly, if the rules of SSP are applied, the employee will only be sick for these purposes if he has a "day of incapacity for work" (incapacity meaning that the employee is unable to perform normal contractual duties because of physical or mental illness or disablement — thus excluding parts of days) and falls within the rules as regards periods of incapacity for work, periods of entitlement, qualifying days, etc.

Medical appointments: In most cases the short duration of a medical appointment will mean that the question of SSP does not arise and so the issue will usually fall to be determined in accordance with the terms of the employee's contract. Many companies will have a set policy on these matters — for instance some employers specifically exclude appointments at the doctor, dentist or optician from the scope of the company sick pay scheme altogether, or will refrain from paying for time off during the week if the matter is not urgent and could be attended to at the weekend. This can be particularly relevant since opticians', doctors' and dentists' surgeries are sometimes open at weekends. However, if there is no provision governing these arrangements it is open to the employer to follow the general definitions contained in the statutory sick pay scheme and decide whether or not the employee is indeed "incapable of work" and entitled to company sick pay or whether the time off does not qualify. Clearly, a distinction must be drawn between, say, a six-monthly check up which may not qualify and hospitalisation for urgent dental, optical or other surgery which will normally be eligible.

In addition, an employer might consider granting time off to allow employees to recuperate from the stresses of work or indeed to assist them to beat a particular addiction. At least one major employer has introduced a facility for time off for those employees who wish to give up smoking to attend courses to assist them to do so.

Health farm visits: An employee's request to take time off work for a visit to a health farm should not normally be treated as sickness *unless* it is on doctor's orders and/or backed up by medical evidence that the employee is "incapable of work". This is unusual as many people visit health farms as much for pleasure as for medical reasons.

However, it is certainly not an impossibility so, again, judgment will need to be exercised in particular cases.

Illness of third parties: Occasionally, situations arise where an employee requests time off work to look after somebody else who has fallen sick. Most commonly this involves members of the family such as a spouse or children but may also concern other relations or friends. In these circumstances the employer is not bound to pay for time off.

Certainly the time off is unlikely to fall under the provisions of a company sick pay scheme and employees will not be eligible for statutory sick pay since it is not the employees themselves who are ill. Such matters are therefore best dealt with as unpaid leave or on a compassionate basis if the illness is serious and/or it is considered appropriate in the circumstances to grant special leave.

Court Appearances

Inevitably, there will be occasions when employees require time off work to attend court in some capacity. They may be required to give evidence in a dispute relating to a workmate's employment, or be prosecuted for a criminal offence. They might even be suing their next-door neighbour over a domestic matter or required to serve as a juror in proceedings brought before a criminal or civil court. All these examples, and others, are bound to lead to employees requesting the employer to release them from work.

Jury service: Under the provisions of the **Juries Act 1974** all men and women aged between 18 and 70 are liable to be summoned by the Lord Chancellor's department to attend for jury service in the Crown Court, the High Court or the County Court, subject to certain limited exceptions or disqualifications. (Those aged 65 or over may be excused.)

Those who are exempted from jury service include people engaged in the legal profession, police officers, certain medical professions, etc. People who have already served on a jury can also be excused.

However, in general, there is a type of "citizen's duty"

on those within the scope of the Act to undertake jury service when summoned and in this respect the Act will override the obligations of an employee to work for the employer during the period of service as a juror. Thus, if employees are required to attend court to undertake jury service the employer is bound to allow them to go. However, the employer is under no legal obligation to agree to pay employees who undertake jury service. It is really a matter of discretion. In any event employees can generally recover compensation for financial losses sustained by them in undertaking jury service (subject to certain prescribed limits) directly from the court.

It is worth noting, however, that if the business would be damaged by an employee's absence on jury service, a letter from the employer to the court, setting out the problems, may result in the employee being excused.

Attending court as a witness: Sometimes an employee can be asked to attend court as a witness in respect of actions brought by third parties and naturally will request time off from the employer. It may be the case, for instance, that the employee is required by the police to give evidence in criminal proceedings or by others involved in litigation — for example an ex-employee who may be pursuing an industrial tribunal claim. In these circumstances, no immediate right to be released from work exists. However, it is not generally advisable to refuse such a request without a very good reason. This is because, at the end of the day, the litigant can seek a court order instructing the witness to attend court (subject to the employer seeking an interlocutory hearing before the court to contest the granting of such an order, for example, if the individual can give no relevant evidence in the proceedings, etc). Once a witness order is served the employer is bound to release the employee from work or face the prospect of being held in contempt of court if it is found that the employer has flagrantly prevented the court's instruction being complied with.

Notwithstanding this, employers are not bound to pay an employee who is attending court in these circumstances, even where the court has ordered the employee to attend. This often comes as something of a shock to those individuals who take the view that, because they have been ordered to attend and therefore have little choice in the matter, naturally their employer should "pick up the bill". This is not so, since equally it is not the employer's fault that they have to attend.

There is one instance where it is desirable to pay employees who attend court as witnesses. This is when the individual has agreed to give evidence on the employer's own behalf. It is quite likely that this will be considered to be a duty carried out in the course of the employment for which the employee must be paid under the terms of the contract. Therefore a failure to compensate the employee in these circumstances may well constitute breach of the contract.

Attendance as defendant or plaintiff: The rules are much the same where the individual is the defendant or the plaintiff in proceedings. Employees who are being prosecuted for a criminal offence or who are being sued on a civil matter must naturally attend court to plead their case. The same applies to individuals who are themselves suing others, even when they are suing their own employer in a case of, say, negligence or in industrial tribunal proceedings, may be for sex or race discrimination, etc. In these circumstances, whilst there is no obligation on the employer to pay for such time off work, realistically it is not open to an employer to refuse to release the employee since, if the court so chooses, it can order the employee's attendance. It should be noted, however, that where individuals are suing their own employer, in many instances it may be possible for them to recover an element of compensation for loss of earnings in bringing the proceedings should they be successful in the action.

Study Leave

Leave of absence for staff to undertake private study is commonly granted in a number of organisations. Again, there is no statutory entitlement here and, unless the contract specifically provides for such time off, employees may be asked to take these periods out of their holiday entitlement. However, in some cases it may be appropriate to grant additional leave for these purposes — for instance if the course of study being undertaken has a direct bearing on the employee's work and/or examinations are imminent.

An extension of general study leave is the sabbatical which is common in many industries and professions. Here employees are granted an extended period of leave to carry out research or study in a particular field. This can serve two purposes for the employer. Firstly, if the research is relevant to the employee's employment the employer may benefit from the individual's increased expertise. Secondly, sabbatical periods can provide a useful means for people to move into a different environment and "recharge their batteries", thus leading to a greater degree of commitment and better job performance on their return to work. Either way there can be benefits to both parties if the leave is granted.

However, it is of course up to the employer to choose whether or not to grant time off, bearing in mind the needs of the business. In common with any other period of extended leave the most important thing to remember is that clear agreement is reached on the terms under which time off is granted. Some managers get themselves into all sorts of problems in this type of situation, mainly in cases where employees return from leave only to find there is no job available for them as the manager has in the meantime filled the post and is happier with the replacement. In the absence of any provision in the original terms under which the leave is granted pointing out quite specifically that there is no guarantee of continued employment on the individual's return, such action is quite likely to lead to a successful claim of unfair dismissal.

Parental Leave

Paternity leave, ie time off work for expectant fathers on the birth of their child, or leave of absence for those who are about to adopt or have recently adopted children, is often granted by organisations as a special leave entitlement. Unlike its counterpart — maternity leave — there is no statutory entitlement to leave of absence for these purposes and it remains a matter for the employer's discretion (unless, of course, provided for in the contract of employment or collective agreement). It should be noted, however, that the code of practice on the elimination of sex discrimination in employment does recommend that personal leave arrangements are adequate for both sexes and notes that men may need to undertake domestic responsibilities especially at times of childbirth. This, of course, is something that must be considered, although the code itself is not legally binding in this capacity.

The length of time (if any) that is granted by employers, and indeed whether this is paid or unpaid, will therefore vary from one company to the next, but is generally limited to the immediate period before and after the time of confinement or adoption.

Miscellaneous Time Off

Religious holidays: Special leave for employees to observe certain religious festivals may be granted at the employer's discretion. It should be noted that while there is no statutory right to have time off for these purposes, the race relations code of practice also recommends that employers consider whether it is reasonably practicable to adapt working arrangements for the purpose of observance of religious holidays.

Marriage: Employees may also be given special time off when they are getting married. This may be confined to the wedding day itself or be granted for a longer period at the employer's discretion.

Moving house: The problems of moving home will generally mean that time off is required at some point — either for keeping appointments with solicitors, estate agents, housing authorities, etc, or for the purpose of the actual move itself. An employer may therefore consider granting special leave for these purposes as and when it is needed.

Others: Various other popular occasions for which special leave can be granted include time off for Christmas shopping, leave to take part in sporting activities, either on behalf of the company or externally, and time off to carry out other commitments in the community such as donating blood or making collections on behalf of charities.

Precedents

It may be the case that, when reviewing company procedures governing time off for special needs, it becomes apparent that a precedent has been created, quite unintentionally. For example, custom and practice dictate that, say, time off for moving home is always granted on the basis of paid leave for two or three days. If the company wants to change this situation it will be necessary to reach agreement with the workforce. Where a union is recognised the issue will have to be dealt with through negotiations. In other cases a clear statement of policy should be included in employees' terms and conditions of employment and their agreement obtained.

6 Holidays

A major reason for employees taking time off work is their annual leave. While this permitted absence from work is enjoyed by every employee, including managers, it is an aspect of time off work that can cause considerable problems.

Many of these problems stem from the assumption that "we have a right to take our holiday; there must be a law that says we can". The truth of the matter is that in most cases there is no relevant law. The right arises from the contract of employment that was entered into with the employer. However, the contract is often silent on essential matters of detail and it is these which may cause ill feeling between employer and employee.

Statutory, Public or Bank Holidays

It is generally thought that everybody in the United Kingdom has a right to certain holidays which are termed statutory or bank holidays or even public holidays. It comes as some surprise, then, to discover that there are only certain groups of employees who have a statutory right to have these days off work.

In England and Wales there are eight public holidays which are defined in the **Banking and Financial Dealings Act 1971**. This Act obviously applies to banks and not generally to other types of employer. In Scotland and Northern Ireland there are some variations in the days designated by this Act as "bank holidays".

Bank Holidays in England and Wales:
— January 1 (New Year's Day)
— Good Friday*
— Easter Monday
— The first Monday in May
— The last Monday in May
— The last Monday in August
— Christmas Day*
— December 26 if it is not a Sunday
— December 27 when December 25 or 26 is a Sunday.

Bank Holidays in Scotland:
— New Year's Day, if it is not a Sunday, otherwise January 3
— January 2, if it is not a Sunday, otherwise January 3
— Good Friday
— The first Monday in May
— The last Monday in May
— The first Monday in August
— Christmas Day, if it is not a Sunday, otherwise December 26
— December 26, if it is not a Sunday.

Bank Holidays in Northern Ireland:
— January 1 (New Year's Day)
— March 17, if it is not a Sunday, otherwise March 18
— Good Friday*
— Easter Monday
— The first Monday in May
— The last Monday in May
— July 12
— The last Monday in August
— Christmas Day*
— December 26, if it is not a Sunday
— December 27, when December 25 or 26 is a Sunday.

*In England, Wales and Northern Ireland, Good Friday and Christmas Day are public holidays not bank holidays.

The actual dates of these holidays can be automatically changed by Parliament when the holiday falls on a Saturday or Sunday. Extra days can also be declared by Royal Proclamation, for instance days to celebrate royal weddings or royal jubilees.

Many employers use the definition of these bank holidays and adopt them under the contract with employees as their own recognised holidays.

Sources of Terms

In the past the only clear statutory requirement to give holidays with pay were made under the various Wages Orders that regulate particular trades and industries, such as the Retail Non Food Wages Order or the Unlicensed Place of Refreshment Wages Order.

The powers of Wages Councils have now been curtailed so that they are no longer able to set statutory holidays or provide minimum annual holidays and related rules. However, their existence tended to mean that employers under these orders incorporated their terms into all existing contracts. Such contracts therefore cannot be changed without agreement without significant risk of unfair dismissal or breach of contract claims.

There are two other possible sources of authority requiring employers to give and pay bank holidays. These are the Statutory Joint Industrial Councils which make agreements applying to various industries or trade union agreements such as the National Engineering Agreement where the holiday requirements are specified. In these cases employers who have incorporated the terms of the agreement into their employees' contracts are obliged to follow such arrangements.

Very often employers use these national agreements as a kind of guideline on the holiday entitlement levels that they should be giving but do not actually incorporate them into their employees' contracts of employment.

The only other possible sources for the employees' rights to take time off for bank holidays are custom and practice in the company or industry concerned and any express terms, ie written terms, in their contracts of employment.

It would be a strange employer indeed who did not give a certain number of days each year as statutory holidays and, of course, they are also commonly given with basic pay.

The holidays listed in the **Banking and Financial Dealings Act** are nowadays widely accepted as holidays. A county court has ruled that, if there is no written contractual provision or regular usage to the contrary, an hourly paid employee is entitled to take a day's holiday on recognised public holidays without fear of dismissal as an absentee and, if employees are entitled to a guaranteed minimum weekly wage, is entitled to be paid without having to work additional hours in that week.

Practical Problems

The sort of practical problems that arise in relation to statutory holidays are things like: "What happens when you are ill on a bank holiday: can you take it again or what do you get paid, holiday pay or sick pay?"; "What happens to SSP due on a day that is also a bank holiday?"; "Is there a rule about having to be at work on the day before and the day after a bank holiday in order to receive payment?"; "What do I have to pay an employee who is required to work on a bank holiday?"; "Can you tag on statutory holidays to weeks of annual leave?"

This kind of question can only be answered by looking at the custom and practice or express written terms of the contract of employment or incorporated national agreements. In practice these are matters which are often

---

Checklist: Bank Holidays

● Check the written holiday rules if there are any.

● Check the payroll and see if the situation has arisen before and, if so, what the decision was on that occasion.

● See if there is any local or trade custom that covers the particular problem.

● Decide on the basis of operating efficiency and general acceptability to employees.

---

subject to *ad hoc* decisions by managers. A logical path to take when making such decisions might well be as follows.

Practical Answers

When employees are ill on a statutory holiday, should they be paid? It is more than likely that a look at the written statement of terms and conditions will refer to a contractual right to paid holiday leave for this day. It is unlikely to make reference to any rule covering the situation, so on a flat reading of the contractual terms it is most likely that payment for the holiday is a right under the contract and presumably that right to payment will continue for every bank holiday during any long period of absence from work through ill health. However, there may be an express or implied rule that after, say, two or three months' absence from work, no further public holidays are paid.

If, under SSP rules, the statutory holiday is also designated as a qualifying day by agreement between the employee and employer technically, provided it qualifies under the SSP rules, SSP should be paid for that day. Therefore any monies paid for the bank holiday can be used to offset the requirement to pay SSP for that day. So far as retaking statutory holidays when an employee has recovered from illness is concerned, it is unlikely that the contract could be read to give that kind of entitlement. However, the employer can agree to that arrangement if appropriate.

Another vexed question concerns part time workers: do they have a statutory holiday entitlement if they do not normally work on the day the statutory holiday falls? The usual answer is that, unless the contract says otherwise, there is only entitlement to statutory holiday if it is a normal working day. It is, of course, helpful to employers and employees alike to spell out this point.

The widespread rule requiring employees to be at work before and after a statutory holiday in order to qualify for payment has as its main source certain national agreements. However, the rule has no legal basis and so, unless it has the status of custom and practice or it is contained in the contract of employment, it cannot be used to deprive an employee of pay. Similarly, the question of tagging on annual leave to statutory holidays is a matter of company policy only.

Working on Statutory Holidays

Employees in, for instance, the catering trade are frequently required to work on statutory holidays and most employers will have a clear statement to that effect in the contract of employment or in the holiday rules. Wages orders and collective agreements often specify the premium rates that are to be paid for work on that date. These orders and agreements usually go on to require other substitute days to be given with pay in lieu of the statutory holiday worked, but for the vast majority of employers it is the agreement between the parties in the terms of the contract that matters. These arrangements may vary from flat time payment for statutory holiday working to triple time or even more, and in some cases time off in lieu is not given at all. It is a matter for agreement between the parties at the outset of employment or, alternatively, some interim *ad hoc* arrangement should be reached when statutory holiday working is required.

Where the employer requires substitute days to be taken for statutory holidays, for instance in order to plan an orderly production schedule, there is usually a requirement to give advance notice of such changes (within the contract or collective agreement, etc) and of course it is good management practice to do so.

Payment for Statutory Holidays

Finally there is the question of payment. As we have already observed, there is no statutory requirement other than those which were once contained in wages orders for payment of statutory holidays. Usually the employees' contracts of employment give details of payment for these days. The calculation of the payments will depend on the contract and may vary from basic pay, a smaller than basic flat amount, payment at average earnings, payment at basic pay plus shift allowance, etc. It is a good idea to make sure than any statement of terms and conditions of employment or written holiday rules contain precise details of how the payment is calculated.

Taking Annual Holiday

Once again this is an area which is determined largely by the employees' contracts of employment. Most employers (except those who have incorporated national agreements or other clauses into their employees' terms and conditions of employment) are free to give as much or as little entitlement as they like. Recent surveys have shown that entitlement generally ranges between 20 and 30 days, with 25 days being the most common. It is not unusual to see this entitlement increasing with the length of service of the employee concerned.

Virtually every organisation has rules, written or otherwise, about the taking of annual holiday and these are usually set out in a staff handbook, statement of terms and conditions of employment, or posted on the noticeboard. This is sensible because it lessens the risk of problems arising out of unknown, unwritten rules or disputed custom and practice. If disputes over entitlement to annual leave becomes serious, the issue can be taken to the County Court for a decision on the interpretation of the contract's terms. Even if there is nothing in writing, the court will hear oral evidence regarding custom and practice and will determine what is the likely agreement between the parties regarding holiday entitlement. Another possible avenue of complaint is to an industrial tribunal regarding the information about holidays contained in the terms and conditions statement. A tribunal has powers to define the terms that amount to custom and practice.

Entitlement

It is important to know what entitlement system the company operates. There are two main types:

- historical accrual system
- current entitlement system.

The former is the system where an employee is required to work an entire year, accruing paid holiday entitlement to be taken in the next holiday year (this system used to be common under wages orders). No paid leave of absence may be taken during the first year of service. This leap-frogging process continues throughout the period of employment. At termination of employment this means that there is a substantial accrued holiday entitlement to be paid in lieu when the employee leaves. However, it is common for employers to allow paid holiday to be taken in advance of entitlement.

The latter is a more common form of holiday entitlement. It allows paid leave during the first year of service, which is calculated pro rata to the period of employment during that year. For instance, someone starting in July, with a holiday year running from January to December is given an entitlement of half their annual entitlement in the first holiday year. This may mean that employees who stay for only a short time take more holiday than they are entitled to receive on leaving employment; it is sensible to ensure there is a company rule stating that such overpayment can be deducted from any monies due on termination. It is also important to know precisely the date when the holiday year commences — eg January 1, April 6, etc.

Part Time Staff

Another area of contention is the holiday entitlement for part time employees and temporary staff. All too often there is nothing in writing regarding their entitlement to paid or unpaid holiday with the result that disputes are not uncommon. The most sensible policy is to ensure that part time staff are treated on a pro rata basis to full time employees. Care must be taken not to fall foul of the **Equal Pay Act**, particularly with part-timers. If such workers are women and they do not receive holiday entitlement on a pro rata basis to their full time male counterparts, they could make a successful claim for equal pay — benefits in kind are treated as pay.

Other Rules

It is generally accepted that holiday entitlement is taken subject to the approval of the employer and it makes sense that such a rule should be stated in writing with all the other holiday rules. Such rules may specify how far in advance requests for leave must be made, to whom and how many people in the same department can be away at any given time. There may be restrictions on the amount of holiday that can be taken at any one time, or at a particular time of year. Sometimes there is a requirement to keep back annual leave to cover shutdown periods when all staff are normally required to be away from work.

It is not uncommon for employees within the same department to have conflicting holiday requirements and it may be necessary for the manager to decide which person's leave will be approved. It would be sensible to define what policy is to operate, ie is priority given to senior employees, to those with longest service, to the person whose request was received first? In tackling such a problem, the best starting point is to ask the conflicting employees to go away and try to solve it between themselves. If that proves to be impossible, the manager must come to a decision. When holiday has to be refused it is sensible to anticipate the possibility of the employee going absent anyway. It is therefore advisable to write a letter to the disappointed employee explaining why the holiday leave has been refused and perhaps giving other dates which would be convenient. It might be pointed out that, if the employee is absent during the period initially requested, a medical certificate for sickness absence during that period will be subject to close investigation and, if it is discovered that the employee did go on holiday, depending on the company's disciplinary procedure, this may be treated as gross misconduct.

Some flexibility in approach is advisable to cope with genuine emergencies: for instance, an unexpected problem at home may occur causing an employee to ask urgently for a few days' holiday to sort the matter out. A too rigid adherence to the rules requiring, say, two or three weeks' notice of intention to take holiday in such circumstances is likely to alienate a normally responsible employee.

Payment of Annual Holiday

Nothing upsets people more than if their holiday pay is not as much as they expected and it is sensible to make sure that the rate of payment for holidays is clearly understood by all employees. For instance, is basic pay the only payment received, or is it calculated on average earnings, on average piece work or some other calculation? Are attendance bonuses included? Very often before a period of annual leave, holiday pay paid in cash is made up in advance and paid together with payment for the preceding week.

What happens to holiday entitlement that is not taken? Can payment in lieu be given? Once again this is completely dependent on the employer's policy and any rules that are in existence. As a matter of good personnel policy it is sensible to encourage employees to take all their holiday entitlement rather than convert a substantial proportion to cash. After all, its basic purpose is to give employees a chance to "recharge their batteries" rather than to "earn" additional money.

Sickness and Holidays

What happens if employees fall ill while they are on holiday? There are essentially two possible courses of action:

● the absence is treated as sickness and the employee is allowed to take time off as holiday again at a later date; or

● it is taken off the employee's holiday entitlement regardless of the illness or any other circumstance.

Very often employers prefer to use their discretion and look at individual cases. Again, subject to any rules, it is up to the employer to decide how to deal with this situation.

This particular problem has been highlighted by the operation of statutory sick pay. Unless any specific provision has been made to the contrary, days of annual holiday will also be qualifying days and consequently, subject to the rest of the rules of SSP, there will be an entitlement to SSP payment. The regulations also require SSP to be offset against any payment made under the employment contract for that particular period of time. As a result SSP can be claimed whilst at the same time the employee "clocks off" holiday leave entitlement without contravening any law. The only thing to be wary about is that if sickness occurs during a holiday outside the EC the employee is excluded from SSP.

Another point of contention arises when employees are away for long periods due to ill-health. Do employees continue to accrue holiday entitlement and are they entitled to take it when they return from the absence? Additionally, can this holiday entitlement be carried over into the next year if it cannot all be taken in the current holiday year?

Under most holiday rules the employee will continue to accrue entitlement in spite of being away ill. A possible exception is where holiday entitlement accrues on the basis of weeks worked, otherwise it will accrue on the basis of weeks of continuous employment and that means whether the employee works or not, unless the employer's rules provide differently. The employer is free to state as a term of the contract that no entitlement can be carried forward to the next year and therefore it is forfeited. Of course, if the employee is dismissed during the year on grounds of ill-health, the usual payment of accrued holiday pay will have to be made (see below).

Leaving Employment

Most employers operate a system whereby holiday is accrued on the basis of so much for each completed month of service in the holiday year. When employees leave for any reason, outstanding holiday earned but not taken is reimbursed to them in the form of pay, less NI contributions and tax deductions. If employees have taken more holiday than they are entitled to, this cannot be deducted from any monies owing unless the terms and conditions of employment relating to holidays make specific provision allowing the employer to do so. It is also possible to have rules that prevent employees from receiving accrued holiday pay if they are dismissed for gross misconduct or if they leave employment without giving the due notice. Once again this must be covered by a specific rule, preferably set down in writing.

Female employees going on maternity leave are often treated as if they are leaving and accrued holiday pay is calculated and paid to them. The law does not oblige employers to count maternity leave for the purposes of holiday accrual, but if the employment continues during the maternity leave period and nothing is said to the contrary, it is possible for courts to imply that the period counts as service and therefore holiday is accruing because the employer has no special rules covering the situation. A sensible step is to ensure that there is a clear company holiday rule in relation to this circumstance.

Taking Holiday while under Notice

Sometimes an employee may ask to take the balance of accrued holiday during the notice period. This may be welcomed by the employer because it prevents the need for additional payments, as the holiday leave will offset the obligation to ensure the person has pay during the notice period. On the other hand it may be extremely inconvenient when a replacement needs to be trained for the leaver's job.

In this situation the usual rules apply, ie the holiday must be taken by agreement between the parties. If the employee has booked holiday and has received permission to go on holiday, the employer should not withdraw agreement just because the employee is about to leave. If employees change their minds about when they want to take leave, after having made an arrangement the employer does not have to agree to revert back to these days being working days. Similarly, if there is a shutdown period employees cannot insist on working on those days. Where a shutdown period is a matter of custom and practice these shutdown days will not count as lay off and so will not qualify for a guarantee payment (see page 102).

Returning Late from Holiday

Employees returning late from holiday are presenting ever-increasing problems. It is not unreasonable to expect employees to contact you if they are unexpectedly prevented from returning to work. However, the best course of action to take is:

● try to contact them to establish whether they have returned home and discover the reason for the delay. If no contact can be made a warning letter should be sent to the employees' homes (or wherever reasonable contact might be made) advising them that their absence is unauthorised and they must contact the company immediately to explain the late return. It is sensible to explain that the absence from work will be treated as gross misconduct if there is not a sufficiently good reason for the late return

- when the employee returns hold a disciplinary meeting to try to establish what happened and determine the best ways to investigate any excuses. Investigation is very important

- the employee should be suspended with pay until the investigation is complete. If the employer has reasonable grounds for believing that the excuses do not hold water, ie the outward and return holiday trip was booked in advance and the employee clearly anticipated being late back from leave, the employer has the option of giving warnings or dismissing, depending on the situation.

If you do not intend to accept foreign medical certificates it is very sensible to explain this to employees at the outset of their holidays.

Extended Leave of Absence

Many employees nowadays would like to take their holidays in a large block, thus enabling them to travel long distances around the world, to Australia or India for example. Often they would like further leave tacked on to this period, either paid or unpaid, so that their visits to such far-flung countries are worthwhile.

Employers frequently grant extended leave on the basis that the employee must return on the due date and that failure to do so will result in dismissal or will mean the contract ends by mutual agreement.

It is extremely unlikely that the courts or tribunals will now accept that the ending of the contract is by mutual agreement: even if an employee has signed a form to this effect, a tribunal is likely to hold that if an employee is not allowed to return to work because he or she has arrived back late, there was a dismissal in law. If employees are granted extended leave on the basis that they must return by the due date or face possible disciplinary sanctions, including dismissal, they must be treated as having received a warning. The employer must investigate why the return was delayed and decide whether this is sufficient reason to dismiss the person concerned. It is likely that some employers will refuse to agree to extended leave and insist that employees resign if they wish to go abroad for a lengthy period. Then, when they return, if there is a suitable vacancy, they can be re-engaged. It is important to note that it is unlikely that the employee's continuous service will be broken by this termination, unless it is made clear that there is no guarantee of a position on the employee's return.

Employers should always bear in mind that there is a legal requirement to provide information about holiday entitlement and pay in the statement of terms and conditions of employment covering such matters as the rate of accrual and entitlement — if any — to accrued holiday pay upon the ending of employment. It is also advisable to document any other relevant holiday rules.

7 Lay Offs

While employees themselves are not usually responsible for the number of days lost due to lay off, it is still important to record these figures and to understand the legal and practical consequences of laying off workers due to shortage of work if absences are to be controlled and plant and machinery utilised effectively.

The Legal Rights

There are three main legal issues involved in laying off workers. The first is the rights given to employees by their contracts of employment, the second involves guarantee payments and, finally, those people laid off may become entitled to redundancy payments even when the employer does not intend — or wish — to make them redundant.

The Contractual Position

Employees may be laid off work without pay only if the employer has a clear contractual right to do this. If it is decided to lay people off on full pay (a fairly unusual course of action as regards manual workers) there is no problem: it has been held over many years that, except in rare instances, there is no obligation on employers to provide work so long as employees are paid. In the majority of cases, therefore, employers may only lay off workers if this is provided for in the contract. This raises the following three possibilities.

Lay Off: Three Contractual Possibilities

- there is provision in the contract for employees to be laid off work

- there is nothing at all in the contract about lay off

- there is no written contract.

All of these options beg the question: what is the contract? It need not be a formal written document. It might consist of a statement of written terms and conditions of employment, possibly backed up by a company handbook, collective agreements, letter of appointment, etc.

If there is a contractual right for employers to lay off without pay then, provided the employer follows all of the contractual terms, including such matters as the amount of notice that has to be given and any guaranteed weekly payments, there is no reason why the employees should not be laid off subject to the guarantee pay provisions set out on page 102.

If there is nothing at all in the contract about lay off, or if there is nothing in writing which sets down the contractual terms, it will be lawful only in the following two circumstances:

● where it is custom and practice in the trade or industry concerned that workers be laid off without pay. The phrase "custom and practice" requires the custom to be reasonable, certain (ie it must be obvious to employer and employees what rights and obligations it imposes on each of them) and it must be well known in the industry or area in which it is said to exist

● if the employees have agreed to be laid off. This is not as rare as it might seem since many people would prefer to have a few weeks' unpaid leave, or to be paid for, say, only three days a week for a time, than to be made redundant and so become unemployed. It is, however, important to note than each individual concerned must consent: it is not sufficient to make an agreement only with the recognised union concerned as, in the vast majority of cases, the union will not have the right to vary employees' contracts in a way that is to their detriment. The reasoning behind these provisions is quite simple — when employees are offered a job, and they accept it, a contract of employment comes into being automatically. In the absence of specific provisions to the contrary the main terms of the contract will state that the employee agrees to work for, say, 38 hours a week and the employer agrees to pay for that number of hours. Provided the employee is available and willing to work for those contractual hours, employers will be acting in breach of contract if they do not pay.

Breach of contract: If the employer does act in breach of employees' contracts they will have two potential forms of redress. Firstly, they could make a claim to a County Court for damages in respect of the employer's breach. Their claim would be for an amount of money equivalent to that which they would have earned had they been allowed to work for their normal weekly hours. Secondly — and this may be as an alternative or in addition to their County Court claim — they may leave and claim that they have been constructively dismissed.

Constructive dismissal arises when an employee resigns, either with or without notice but in circumstances when he or she is entitled to leave without notice because of the employer's conduct. What this means in practice is that an employee who resigns is treated in law as having been dismissed if the resignation was based directly on the fact that the employer acted in fundamental breach of an important term of the contract. There can be little doubt that pay *is* an important term of the contract and, where the loss of earnings is significant, it is most likely to constitute a fundamental breach.

It is clear, then, that failure to pay employees their wages for a period, without a contractual right to do so, is almost certain to constitute constructive dismissal, thus enabling the employees concerned to leave and make an unfair dismissal claim to an industrial tribunal. This is not to say, however, that their claim will succeed automatically. While the fact of the dismissal, in law, is unlikely to be in doubt, the employer may still defend the fairness of the dismissal.

While it is true that such claims are more difficult for employers to defend than most unfair dismissal claims there will be circumstances where it would be possible. For instance, in the situation mentioned above when agreement from the employees has to be sought, if all employees except one agree to be laid off and it is known that they would withdraw their agreement if that one person continued to work or to be paid in full, a subsequent constructive dismissal may be held to be fair. This would not prevent the employee making a successful County Court claim and so, in such circumstances, it would be better to grasp the nettle, dismiss the employee concerned after going through a fair procedure (eg full consultation, warnings as to the result of continued refusal to agree to lay off, etc) and give normal notice of the termination.

Constructive dismissal might also arise where the lay off is prolonged — there will come a point when a tribunal could hold that the contractual right to lay off means to lay off for a "reasonable" period and the employer has kept employees laid off for an unreasonable length of time.

Redundancy Payments

Even where there is a contractual right to lay off employees, or their agreement has been obtained to lay them off for a period, they may, after a certain time, be able to leave and claim a redundancy payment. The rules governing this provision are extremely complex. In essence, they provide that employees may begin the procedure for making a claim when:

- they are laid off (ie no work is provided for a week and so no payments are made)

- they are kept on short time working to the extent that they receive less than half the amount of a normal week's pay because of a shortage of work

- for four or more consecutive weeks or for a series of six or more weeks, of which not more than three are consecutive, in a period of 13 weeks.

If employees' circumstances fit within these factors, the following procedure must be followed.

- They must serve a notice on their employer setting out their intention to claim a redundancy payment within four weeks of the end of the period set out above.

- The employer may defeat the claim by serving on the employees, within seven days, a counter-notice stating that on the date the employees' notice was served it was reasonably to be expected that, within four weeks, normal working would resume and would continue without further lay off or short time working for a further 13 weeks.

- If no such counter-notice is served, the employees must give due notice to terminate the employment within four weeks of sending the notice of their intention to claim.

- If the employer gives a counter-notice but withdraws it in writing, the employees must give notice within three weeks of the notice of withdrawal.

- If the employer gives a counter-notice and does not withdraw it, the employees must make a claim to an industrial tribunal and within three weeks of the date on which they are notified of the tribunal's decision they must give notice to terminate their employment.

These provisions do not apply to any weeks of lay off or short time working which are due to a strike or lock-out, regardless of the industry or even country in which the dispute occurs. Thus, workers in a vehicle assembly factory in Britain who were laid off due to a strike in a manufacturer of components in, say, Germany could not rely on these provisions to claim redundancy payments, although their contractual rights would not be affected by the cause of the lay off.

It should be noted that redundancy rights in this situation would not be lost if the shortage of work was caused by a work-to-rule or an overtime ban elsewhere — the action must constitute a stoppage of work. Equally, the fact that employers decided to dismiss workers on grounds of a shortage of work due to a strike or lock-out elsewhere would not disentitle them to a redundancy payment.

Calculating Redundancy Payments

Redundancy payments are based on the age and length of service of employees. Working backwards from the date the employee leaves (or, if full notice was not given, the date the statutory notice would have expired), the calculation is as follows: (the maximum number of years which can be taken into account is 20):

- for each year of employment when the employee is 41 years or over, one and a half week's pay

- for each year when the employee is 22 or over, one week's pay

- for each year when the employee is at least 18, half a week's pay.

There is a statutory limit on the amount of a week's pay. This is currently (from April 1992) £205. The maximum redundancy payment is thus $1^1/_2$ x 20 x £205 = £6150.

However, if the contract terminates when the employee is between the ages of 64 and 65, this amount is reduced by $1/_{12}$th for each complete month of employment after the 64th birthday, so that no redundancy payments are due for women or men over 65 years.

Where the company's normal retirement age is less than 65 years, this age acts as the cut-off point for receiving redundancy pay, but in some cases there is no reduction of the amount in respect of the final year before retirement.

Guarantee Payments

In addition to their rights under contract and to possible rights to leave and claim redundancy payments, employees who are laid off work must be paid statutory guarantee payments.

The right to receive such payments arises when employees are provided with no work by the employer, on a day when they would normally be required to work, because of a shortage of the work they are employed to do or because of any other occurrence affecting the normal operation of the business.

However, this right is subject to certain limitations:

- it applies only to employees who work for at least 16 hours a week and who have been continuously employed for at least one month (employees who work for at least eight but less than 16 hours a week become entitled when they have been employed for five years)

- it is lost if the reason for the lay off is an industrial dispute involving employees of the employer or of an associated employer, even if the employees to be laid off have nothing to do with the dispute

- if employees are offered suitable alternative employment, but refuse it, the right is again lost

- similarly, the right is lost if employees refuse to comply with reasonable requirements imposed by the employer with a view to ensuring that their services are available. For instance, if employees turn up to work and find there is nothing they can do because there is a power cut, they are likely to lose entitlement to guarantee pay if they refuse to comply with a request from their employer to wait on site for an hour or two to see if power is restored.

It should also be noted that there must be no work at all done on the day for a statutory guarantee payment to become payable. Thus, if employees begin to work but have to stop after a few hours because of late delivery of components and are then sent home, no guarantee pay will be due (although employees' contractual rights will not be affected).

The entitlement to be paid guarantee pay means an entitlement to be paid for the first five workless days in each three month period at the normal daily rate of pay or at the rate of £14.10 a day (from April 1992), whichever is the lower amount. This figure is usually uprated each year. The calculations necessary to determine the appropriate amount are:

Guarantee payment = number of normal working hours on the day in question x guaranteed hourly rate.

"Normal working hours" mean, broadly, the hours during which the employee is contractually required to be at work.

The guaranteed hourly rate (ghr) is calculated according to the following formula:

$$ghr = \frac{\text{one week's pay}}{\text{number of normal working hours in a week for that employee under the contract of employment in force on the workless day.}}$$

There are two exceptions. Where the number of normal working hours varies from week to week, the guaranteed hourly rate is calculated as follows:

$$ghr = \frac{\text{one week's pay x 12}}{\text{number of the employee's normal working hours during the 12 week period ending with the last complete week before the workless day.}}$$

However, any contractual pay which has to be made in respect of workless days may be offset against the liability to pay guarantee payments. For instance, if there is a contractual obligation to pay employees £6 for each workless day for the first five such days in a three month period, employees would have to be paid the £6 under their contracts plus the balance of £8.10 to make up the guarantee payment (assuming their normal daily rate was more than £14.10).

Where contractual pay is paid on a weekly basis the situation is slightly different. Take the example of an employee who is guaranteed a payment of £100 a week for 40 hours, and works for four days and is laid off on the fifth but is entitled to £110 for the 32 hours worked. Contractually he or she is entitled to no guarantee pay for that week but will be entitled to a full statutory guarantee payment for the workless day. Alternatively, suppose that he or she had only been entitled to £95 for the work actually done. The make-up on the contractual guarantee would be £5 and that amount could be set against the statutory liability for the fifth day. Thirdly, suppose that the employee was contractually entitled to £95 for three days and there were two workless days, the make up of £5 would be apportioned for these purposes equally between the two workless days. If the employer was only bound to pay a guarantee payment for one of those days the full payment less £2.50 would be due.

The Practical Issues

In addition to employees' rights under the foregoing provisions, there are practical implications to laying people off work. In particular, the effects on employees' morale — and consequently efficiency and commitment to the organisation — should be considered as should methods of reducing financial hardships faced by them.

Minimising Lay Offs

Wherever possible, it is obviously in the organisation's interest to minimise the frequency and length of periods of lay off and short time working. Not only do such periods require the same expenditure on overheads for nil production but they can also have a serious effect on morale. They are often seen by employees as a forerunner to cutbacks and factory closures and so are likely to result in the best employees — in terms of skills, ability, etc — looking elsewhere for jobs.

It is therefore sensible to carry out some forward planning so that, whenever possible, difficulties are foreseen in advance and appropriate measures, such as bans on overtime and recruitment, retirement of those people over retirement age, etc are taken before layoffs become necessary.

Minimising the Financial Difficulties

Of course, with the best will in the world, it is not always possible to avoid the necessity of laying off employees or at least reducing the number of hours they are required to work each week for a period. In such a situation the employer can at least try to minimise the financial impact on the employees concerned by choosing a pattern of lay off which maximise the possibility of them claiming benefits from the State.

Unemployment Benefit: Provided employees are entitled to receive this benefit, it is payable in respect of "any day of unemployment which forms part of a period of interruption of employment''. An interruption of employment means at least two days (whether or not consecutive) of unemployment in any six consecutive days (not including Sundays). Thus, employees working a normal week of 40 hours might be better off if they were laid off for two days in alternate weeks than if their working hours were reduced by $1^1/_2$ hours per day. However, this would mean employers having to pay guarantee payments for the first five workless days and, because they had received these payments, employees would not be eligible for unemployment benefit for those days. When setting the pattern of lay off it is also worth remembering that benefit is not payable where a person earns an amount equal to or above the lower earnings limit for NI contributions.

Full details about unemployment benefit and other benefits which employees may be able to claim in lay off situations are contained in *Croner's Reference Book for Employers* and in leaflets issued by the DSS which are obtainable from any local office.

8   Other Absences

Finally, we turn to absence from work for three further reasons, one involuntary, the other two less so:

- suspension from work on medical grounds;
- disciplinary suspension;
- and absence due to imprisonment.

Suspension on Medical Grounds

The first point to make about medical suspension in this context is that it has nothing to do with sickness absence. Indeed, people who are suspended on medical grounds feel perfectly fit and healthy but, if they were not suspended, they would run the risk of over-exposure to radiation or to absorption of dangerous levels of lead, etc.

The provisions governing suspension from work on medical grounds are contained in the **Employment Protection (Consolidation) Act 1978** (as amended). This provides that employees who are suspended in accordance with:

- The Control of Substances Hazardous to Health Regulations 1988
- The Ionising Radiations Regulations 1985
- The Control of Lead at Work Regulations 1980

and who work for at least 16 hours a week and have been employed for at least a month (or who work for less than 16 but at least eight hours a week and have been employed for at least five years) are entitled to be paid, at their normal weekly rate, for up to 26 weeks.

However, the right to paid suspension on medical grounds is lost in the following three situations:

- if the employee is incapable of work due to illness, injury or disablement (in which case occupational sick pay, SSP, NI sickness benefit or invalidity benefit, as appropriate, would be payable)

- if the employee is offered alternative work which it would be reasonable for him or her to do in terms of factors such as health and safety, capability, status, etc and he or she unreasonably refuses to perform that work

- if the employee refuses to comply with reasonable requirements imposed by the employer with a view to ensuring that his or her services are available — eg telephoning the employer on a weekly basis to check whether alternative work has become available.

It should be noted that employees who are suspended from work on medical grounds and who are dismissed for that reason, have the right to make an application to an industrial tribunal claiming that they have been unfairly dismissed, subject to the qualifying service of only one month.

Disciplinary Suspension

Employees may be subject to unpaid suspension from work on disciplinary grounds. However, there are three important points to note in this respect:

Contractual rights: The contractual provisions surrounding suspensions on disciplinary grounds are the same as those that govern lay off (see page 97). If the employer has not reserved the right in the contract to suspend employees without pay, such suspensions may lead to claims of breach of contract in the County Courts or applications to industrial tribunals.

Making the punishment effective: Even if employees' contracts of employment contain an express clause giving the employer the right to suspend them without pay for certain disciplinary offences, it is important that such a penalty is likely to be effective. The whole point of disciplinary sanctions should be to deter employees from behaving in contravention of the rules.

ACAS code: There is a code of practice, prepared by the Advisory Conciliation and Arbitration Service, on Disciplinary Practice and Procedures in Employment. This code and the recommendations it contains are not binding on employers but failure to follow its recommendations may be taken into account. On the subject of disciplinary suspensions the code says:

> *"The final step (of a disciplinary procedure) might be . . . disciplinary suspension without pay (but only if allowed for by an express or implied condition of the contract of employment) . . . . Special consideration should be given before imposing disciplinary suspension without pay and it should not normally be for a prolonged period."*

It is important to note that disciplinary suspension without pay as a penalty should be imposed only after a full investigation has been carried out and a disciplinary meeting held — the suspension will then be imposed as the penalty. Unpaid suspension should not be used when it is considered necessary to remove an employee from the premises whilst a potential disciplinary offence is investigated. To do so would be to prejudge the issue and impose a punishment before the employee had had the chance to give his or her side of the story. In such situations, employees should be suspended on full pay.

Imprisonment

People who are imprisoned are obviously going to be unable to attend work. There is a temptation for some employers to regard this as sufficient reason to dismiss but caution is advisable. For instance, if an employee is being held on remand he or she may be released on bail and be able to resume work; or it might be the case that he or she has been sentenced for a very short term; or is about to appeal and has a reasonable prospect of being successful, and so on and so on.

Employees who are dismissed because they are imprisoned will have a strong prospect of making a successful claim of unfair dismissal if they will be in prison for a relatively short period of time and an employee would not be dismissed for absence of a similar length for other reasons, such as sickness. This, of course, is subject to the proviso that the offence for which they were sentenced to imprisonment does not make their continued employment impossible — as might be the case for instance if an accountant was convicted of embezzlement. However, even where the alleged crime does affect the employer's trust in the employee or impinges on the employment relationship in some other way, the employer should consider the matter carefully and give the employee a chance to have a say (perhaps through a solicitor, or by letter) before deciding to dismiss.

It might be possible to argue that a contract of employment was frustrated by imprisonment. This, however, can present problems since it involves technical legal concepts. Frustration only arises when an event, which could not have been foreseen at the outset of the contract, occurs without either party to the contract being at fault and makes future performance of the contract impossible or radically different from that which was envisaged. If a contract is frustrated it comes to an end automatically — there is no dismissal and so no need for notice and the employee would have no unfair dismissal rights. Such a situation might arise when an employee is given a long sentence or where the sentence is long in relation to the expected duration of the contract. In one case, for example, an apprenticeship agreement was held to have been frustrated when the apprentice was sent to Borstal for six months as a result of his involvement in a gang fight (outside working hours). In most cases, though, it is safer for the employer to give the matter careful consideration and decide whether the employee's absence due to imprisonment amounts to reasonable grounds for dismissal, rather than relying on the possibility of frustration.

If it is decided that the person will remain in employment, no question of wages or salary should arise; the contractual position is that, as the employee is not able to carry out the work, the employer is under no obligation to pay.

Further Information

Could You Use Additional Copies of this Book?

Croner's Guide to Managing Absence is a pocket book designed for practical use by all those with management responsibilities. If you are a subscriber to *Croner's Reference Book for Employers* this is the fourth free book on key areas of employment.

Are there other managers in your organisation who would benefit from having a copy to hand? Are you currently training your managers to handle dismissal fairly? If so, why not give them a copy to help them consolidate their knowledge and put into practice what they have learnt.

Additional copies at a special price of £5 plus £1 p+p per copy may be ordered by telephoning our Customer Services team on 081-547 3333 quoting reference KCMM.

Other books

You may not be aware of the many books we publish on subjects of interest and relevance to employers. The broad range of topics covered reflects the breadth of your responsibilities and interests.

Our books always take a practical approach and are written with the non-specialist in mind. Jargon-free language, the essential facts and a clear format ensure that these books meet your needs.

Here are some of the titles we publish:

Introduction to Employment Law
by Robert Upex
Price: £19.95
ISBN: 1 85452 063 6

Protecting your Business and Confidential Information
by Audrey Williams
Price: £10.95
ISBN: 1 85524 109 9

Procedure in Industrial Tribunal Cases
by Vivian Du-Feu
Price: £12.95
ISBN: 1 85525 108 0

Collective Labour Law
by Martin Warren
Price: £10.95
ISBN: 1 85524 107 2

**Psychometric Testing in Personnel Selection
and Appraisal**
by Paul Kline
Price: £19.95
ISBN: 1 85524 112 9

The Role of the Pension Fund Trustee
by John Cunliffe
Price: £15.95
ISBN: 1 85524 091 2

Debt Recovery in the County Court
by Michael Barry
Price: £19.95
ISBN: 1 85524 118 8

Dictionary of Payroll Terms
by Derek French
Price: £14.95
ISBN: 1 85524 162 5

For Further details contact our Customer Services team on
081-547 3333 quoting reference SM5.

Conferences and Training

Attending a seminar is one of the best ways of keeping up with rapidly changing legislation, trends and new ideas. Croner Conferences and Training have 10 years experience of running an extensive range of courses, from three-day residential to one-day seminars, all led by authoritative and experienced speakers.

Courses are regularly offered on the following subjects:

Handling Disciplinary Situations and Interviews

The Effective Secretary

Going to Tribunal

Concise Guide to Employment Law

SSP and Controlling Absence

SMP and Other Maternity Rights

The Effective Personnel Assistant

Introduction to Employment Law

Fair Dismissal — The 'Dos and Don'ts'

Employment Law — The European Dimension

Drafting Contracts of Employment

Managing People Effectively

Selection Interviewing

Managing Performance Appraisal

Fleet Management

Occupational Pensions: Current Issues and Choices

Developments in Payroll Management

For further information on any of these courses please contact Elizabeth Wolton on 081-547 3333 quoting reference TD22.

Index